Spoken
Arabic
MADE EASY

**A unique course in spoken
Arabic for beginners.**

AMANULLA VADAKKANGARA

GOODWORD

Goodword Books Pvt. Ltd.
1, Nizamuddin West Market, New Delhi - 110 013
e-mail: info@goodwordbooks.com
First pubished 2006
Reprinted 2007
Printed in India
© Goodword Books 2007

www.goodwordbooks.com

CONTENTS

ABOUT THE AUTHOR

AmanullaVadakkangara was born in Vadakkangara in Malappuram district of Kerala, India. He completed a masters degree in Arabic language and literature from the University of Calicut and a Masters degree in the library and information science from Annamalai University Tamil Nadu.

He was inclined towards writing in his school days and published articles in dailies in Kerala. He taught Arabic and Islamic studies at Ansar English School in Perumpilavu for about five years and for the past Ten years he has been working at the Ideal Indian School, Doha and currently he is the head of the department of the Arabic and Islamic Studies.

In Doha he has been a regular writer and columnist in Arabic and English dailies. He has been awarded the Lokseva award by the Government of India for his work on Alcoholism and the best Islamic Educationist award in 1998 for his articles published in the Doha based English daily, Gulf Times.

Among the authors published works are: Improve your spoken Arabic, A literary history of the Arabs, Arabic grammar made easy, A formula to speak Arabic, Catastrophes of Alcoholism, After S.S.L.C. What?, Technical terms, Eid Mubarak, Ramadan, Tobacco free sports, Smoking or health: Choice is yours, Together for a drug free society, and Love Revolution through blood donation and healthy environment for children.

Amanulla Vadakkangara
Doha Qatar

PREFACE

Since the Gulf countries give a multitude of openings to the skilled and unskilled, the number of people learning Arabic has tremendously increased. This includes professionals and technicians of various communities. Due to the intensive nationalisation drive in almost all parts of the Gulf it has become essential to learn at least the basics of Arabic language for all those who are aspirant of finding a job in the region.

It is quite natural that these multitude prefer a working knowledge of the language rather going to the details of its towering literary value and excellence. The demand to give a digestible but sustainable interactive course to the beginners of the language was found need of the hour. My Ten years stay in Qatar convinced me the importance of such a short course and I started to teach Arabic to the working people of various non-Arabic speaking communities in Qatar.

More I interacted with people of various strata the more I was enlightened on the areas of great significance to the working people and I could conduct more than two dozen batches of Spoken Arabic Course for the beginners in a short span of time. I was delighted to see the short-term programme enabled the participants to strengthen the foundation of language learning and to communicate with the Arabic Speaking people in a limited sense. Those who attended my course included diplomats of various countries, senior executives, managers, doctors, engineers and a good number of professionals. My students often asked me to recommend any books, which will ease their efforts in learning and serve as a source of reference. This made me think of compiling the course material in the form of a book, which will help thousands of people to improve their working knowledge in the language and help them to understand the Arabic conversation in a simple way.

I discussed the matter with my friends and well wishers and I was overwhelmed with the support from all corners and actually it was the driving force in materialising this book.

I hope this book will help any one with out any basic knowledge of the language to develop self-learning skills and communicate with others. However I feel it would be highly recommended to listen to the alphabet from those who know the language to get the actual pronunciation of words and phrases.

I need not state that perseverance and desire to learn the language should be there to attain the goal. Even though this book is meant for the beginners of the language, I hope there will be some lessons of common interest to the beginners as well as to the advanced levels.

Since the bilinguilism has developed and has made it the basic qualification for any top jobs in the Gulf region, the importance of Arabic language has increased even otherwise Arabic is quite relevant and significant for many reasons.

It is estimated that about 160 million people speak Arabic from the eastern deserts of the Arabian Peninsular to the forests bordering the banks of the Mediterranean Sea, touching the Moroccan shores. The language that they speak occupies such a place of prominence today that an increasing number of people have come forward with various courses to simplify learning the language to those who do not speak it. It is the language of the Arab World, comprising the countries of North Africa, the Fertile Crescent of the Middle East, the Arab Peninsula and the Gulf States. Large numbers of émigrés in communities also speaks Arabic all over the world.

The geopolitical importance of the Arab World is more evident today than ever before. Because of its oil and gas wealth and its strategically important position between Eastern and Western hemispheres. The well paid posts in major oil and gas firms, is the Gulf states which give a better hopes of perks and facilities requires one to have a mastery over Arabic as well as English.

However this book will not be sufficient for those who opt for such posts, but definitely it will give them a clear insight to the language learning process and help them to start learning.

The 600 million Muslims use Arabic all over the world as the liturgical language of Islam. But the importance of this language need not be understood in the limited context of its religious importance. There is no doubt that it is highly important to the Muslims to understand the Quranic teachings and the traditions of the prophet. But apart from its religious significance the international acceptance and relevance are to be underlined. This has made the United Nations, the apex body of international issues to include it among the selected languages of communications.

Greatness of a language is often measured by its capacity to incorporate words from other languages and vice versa. Arabic is a very successful language in this respect and studies show that there are about 1,000 main words of Arabic origin in the English language and many other words derived from Arabic. Arabic words can be found in every area of language use, ranging from the sciences to the arts, to foods and other areas of everyday life.

It is a proved fact that during the Middle Ages (the 8th to 13th centuries) the Arabic speaking people were the main bearers of the torch of knowledge and civilization. Arabic was the medium, through which the science and philosophy of Greece and other ancient civilizations were recovered,

Supplemented and transmitted in such a way as to make possible the European Renaissance in the full sense.

It is important that the student realizes from the start that there are two kinds of Arabic. One is spoken at home, or in the street, but it is not written. The second is spoken in schools and universities, in radio and television, and is written in newspapers and books. But in this book I have freely mixed the spoken and written languages in a pattern of my own so that the learner may be able to follow both in a limited way.

The course is an introduction to Arabic for students with no previous knowledge of the language. It is designed as part of a sequence that will enable the student to understand, , read, write and speak Arabic with ease, with a basic idea of spoken styles and usage of the Arab world.

I have attempted to make it simple and easy to the learners to understand and interact with native Arabs. If determined efforts are made, at the end of the course it is assumed that the student should be able to comprehend and to summarise the basic information (ideas, arguments, themes, issues) of almost any Arabic conversation, whether printed or spoken, and also to initiate and take part in simple and serious conversations with educated Arabs, to reproduce and appropriately modify patterns of simple spoken Arabic. To read through and understand written texts of moderate difficulty. To write simple but correct and accurate Arabic.

Arabic is one of the most simplest languages of the world. If imparted properly any body blessed with a flair for language learning can master it without much difficulty.

As there are certain letters special to Arabic language learners may face difficulty in hearing or reproducing certain sounds. It is essential that a student should have enough listening practices before he proceed with learning phrases and communication tools to follow correct pronunciation. Concerted efforts to reproduce the sounds as frequently as possible are also highly essential. This will be more with regard to some special letters, which are unique in Arabic. In this case I have tried my level best to avoid such special letters to the maximum possible and made the learner feel ease and comfort.

The second difficulty is writing. Arabic has a very different alphabet from Latin. Letters have different forms, at the beginning, middle or end of a word. To complicate things still more, short vowels are not written. In order to overcome this difficulty, the student is encouraged to write and rewrite texts and exercises and make sure that he or she knows it well. Writing always goes hand in hand with reading and hearing; continued practice is essential.

The third difficulty, which is not necessarily peculiar to Arabic, is how to reach a level of fluency that allows students to conduct a simple conversation. The best way to overcome this difficulty is to possess right from the beginning a variety of useful expressions, and to practice the use of various conversational patterns in day to day dealings.

As far as a beginner is concerned it is not necessary that he must be thorough with all parts of speech and grammatical lessons rather he is advised to acquire a working knowledge of the language to communicate with people.

When he starts communicating he will realise his requirements and he can refer to the necessary parts for additional knowledge.

I have given some model conversations, which can be the base for any one to build up a conversation of his own. A number of questions and answers are also added to facilitate learners to express themselves on various occasions.

The selected past and present tense forms as well as the

opposites will be useful not only to find out how words are joined or made in to the desired patterns but also to improve spoken skills by coining the right word at the right occasion.

The dictionary part attached at the end of the book will definitely help every one for finding words of their choice.

While bringing out this book I have to record my heartfelt thanks and gratitude all my friends and well wishers for their unqualified support. I am thankful to the Editorial team of Qatar's prominent English daily, Gulf Times for their support and encouragement to all my activities.

I am really indebted to my former principals at the Ideal Indian School, Dr. T. K. Mohammed and Mr. Ainsley Edgar for their creative support and motivation.

My special thanks are due to my colleagues at the Ideal Indian School. I place on record my gratitude to all members of managing committee and founder members council of Ideal Indian School for all their kind support and patronage.

I express my sincere thanks to my brother Jouhar who typed the whole text.

With these words let me submit this before the learners and readers. My request is to point out errors and mistakes, if any and assure that suggestions and creative evaluations will be highly appreciated and looked in to while modifying the book.

Amanulla Vadakkangara
Doha Qatar

LESSON ONE

ARABIC ALPHABET

ح	ج	ث	ت	ب	ا
س	ز	ر	ذ	د	خ
ع	ظ	ط	ض	ص	ش
م	ل	ك	ق	ف	غ
	ي	و	هـ	ن	

Unlike many languages Arabic is written from right to left. Scholars who have conducted extensive research on the language scripts observe that writing from right to left refers to the greatness of the language as there are several advantages in this way. First of all we all prefer to do any good action with our right. Secondly when we write from right to left the energy spent is far lesser than we spent to write from left to right as the energy to pull and push varies.

Also if some one is writing on the board in writing left to write there is possibility of covering the part written earlier while moving towards the right, where as while writing from right to left more he writes the more will be clear to the students. However I feel the greatness of the Arabic letters lies in its capacity to carry various vowels and produce different sounds from the same original letter.

There are 28 letters in Arabic. Each letter can carry three vowels and we can make 84 sounds from the alphabet. Vowel in Arabic is called Harakah and the three conditions of Harakah are:

Fathhah, Kasrah and Dammah.

Fathah: A small diagonal stroke above a consonant. It is identical with vowel ' a' in man.

Kasrah: A small diagonal stroke under a consonant. It is identical with vowel ' i' in the English word 'tin'.

Dammah: A small waw above a consonant. It is identical with vowel 'u' in the English word 'pull'.

If a consonant is without a vowel we put a small zero above the letter. That is called sukoon.

The alphabet with different vowels are shown below:

أْ	U أُ	E إِ	A أَ	ا
بْ	بُ	بِ	بَ	ب
تْ	تُ	تِ	تَ	ت
ثْ	ثُ	ثِ	ثَ	ث

14

جْ	جُ	جِ	جَ	ج
حْ	حُ	حِ	حَ	ح
خْ	خُ	خِ	خَ	خ
دْ	دُ	دِ	دَ	د
ذْ	ذُ	ذِ	ذَ	ذ
رْ	رُ	رِ	رَ	ر
زْ	زُ	زِ	زَ	ز
سْ	سُ	سِ	سَ	س
شْ	شُ	شِ	شَ	ش
صْ	صُ	صِ	صَ	ص
ضْ	ضُ	ضِ	ضَ	ض
طْ	طُ	طِ	طَ	ط
ظْ	ظُ	ظِ	ظَ	ظ
عْ	عُ	عِ	عَ	ع

غْ	غُ	غِ	غَ	غ
فْ	فُ	فِ	فَ	ف
قْ	قُ	قِ	قَ	ق
كْ	كُ	كِ	كَ	ك
لْ	لُ	لِ	لَ	ل
مْ	مُ	مِ	مَ	م
نْ	نُ	نِ	نَ	ن
هْـ	هُـ	هِـ	هَـ	هـ
وْ	وُ	وِ	وَ	و
يْ	يُ	يِ	يَ	ي

LONG VOWELS

The Arabic letters a, wa and ya which are described by the grammarians as weak or irregular letters are used for lengthening the vowels. It is important to note that when these letters are used for lengthening the sound they do not carry any vowels.

How the sound of the letters are extended is given below:

و + أُ   ي + إِ   ا + أَ

16

و + بُ	ي + بِ	ا + بَ
و + تُ	ي + تِ	ا + تَ
و + ثُ	ي + ثِ	ا + ثَ
و + جُ	ي + جِ	ا + جَ
و + حُ	ي + حِ	ا + حَ
و + خُ	ي + خِ	ا + خَ
و + دُ	ي + دِ	ا + دَ
و + ذُ	ي + ذِ	ا + ذَ
و + رُ	ي + رِ	ا + رَ
و + زُ	ي + زِ	ا + زَ
و + سُ	ي + سِ	ا + سَ
و + شُ	ي + شِ	ا + شَ
و + صُ	ي + صِ	ا + صَ

و + ضُ	ي + ضِ	ا + ضَ
و + طُ	ي + طِ	ا + طَ
و + ظُ	ي + ظِ	ا + ظَ
و + عُ	ي + عِ	ا + عَ
و + غُ	ي + غِ	ا + غَ
و + فُ	ي + فِ	ا + فَ
و + قُ	ي + قِ	ا + قَ
و + كُ	ي + كِ	ا + كَ
و + لُ	ي + لِ	ا + لَ
و + مُ	ي + مِ	ا + مَ
و + نُ	ي + نِ	ا + نَ
و + هُـ	ي + هِـ	ا + هَـ

و + اُ   ي + وِ   ا + وَ

و + يُ   ي + يِ   ا + يَ

NUNATION

Nouns and adjectives, when indefinite, the vowel signs are written double. This is called nunation. In spoken language very often these are not pronounced as the vowel of the last letter is not made clear .

For example: Walad (ولد)can be pronounced as walad, even though the actual pronunciation is waladun .

DOUBLE CONSONANT

When a consonant occurs double, a special symbol is put on the letter. This is called the doubling symbol. In English, the doubling is used for stress as well as for extension of the sound but in Arabic it is used only for stress.

Example: مُ حَ مَ د

After this brief introduction now we can start forming words. The world of Arabic words is so exciting. Observe the words given below closely and try to learn reading and writing of these words and understand its meaning.

LESSON TWO

FORMATION OF WORDS

As we are thorough with the Arabic alphabet, now we can form simple words. A list of words given below will give the learner a clear idea regarding reading and writing of simple Arabic words.

Father	Abun	اب
Brother	Akhun	اخ
Pain	Alamun	ا ل م
Son	Ibnun	ا ب ن
Sin	Ithmun	اث م
Name	Ismun	ا س م
Mother	Ummun	ام
Sister	Ukhtun	ا خ ت
Family	Usratun	ا س ر ة
Cow	Baqaratun	ب ق ر ة
Sea	Bahrun	ب ح ر
Well	Bi'run	ب ء ر
Girl	Bintun	ب ن ت
Dates	Tamrun	ت م ر
Ox	Thaurun	ث و ر

Let us also see some words with long vowels.

Residence	Iqama	ا ق ا م ة
Leave	Ijaza	ا ج ا ز ة
Door	Babun	ب ا ب
Garden	Bustanun	ب س ت ا ن
Orange	Burtuqal	ب ر ت ق ا ل
Student	Tilmeedun	ت ل م ي ذ

Now we can read any word with long or short vowels. Excellence in the language greatly depends upon the vocabulary one possesses and the learner is recommended to learn as many words as possible.

JOINING

Until now we have been dealing with detached words only. But in our actual language usage we do not find detached words at all. All words are joined and a learner should know basically how to join words.

Joining is very simple. We need to abide by the following instructions.

1. There are six non-connecting letters. They are:

ا د ذ ر ز و

We can not join any letters immediately after these non connecting letters.

2. While joining we have to cut the down part of the letters unless it is the last letter. Last letter will appear completely.

3. As the dots are inevitable part of the letter we can not cut the dots. In such cases we will cut the first part of the letter.

Now see how the following words are joined as per the guidelines given.

School	Madrasatun	مدرسة	م د ر س ة
Chair	Kursee	كرسي	ك ر س ي
Garden	Hadeeqa	حديقة	ح د ي ق ة
Animal	Hayawan	حيوان	ح ي و ا ن
Man	Insan	انسان	ا ن س ا ن
Bag	Haqeebah	حقيبة	ح ق ي ب ة
Effort	Muhawala	محاولة	م ح ا و ل ة
Interview	Muqabala	مقابلة	م ق ا ب ل ة
Discussion	Munaqasha	مناقشة	م ن ا ق ش ة

LESSON THREE

SENTENCE FORMATION

We have seen how to make words and write them in both detached and joined ways. Now let us try to form simple nominal sentences. To facilitate this I shall introduce certain demonstrative pronouns here.

This (M)	*hada*	هذا
This (F)	*hadihi*	هذه
That (M)	*dalika*	ذلك
That (F)	*tilka*	تلك

Once we learn these demonstrative pronouns we can easily put them together with nouns we have learned earlier to form sentences. Some examples are given below.

This is a pen	*hada qalamun*	هذا قلم
This is a book	*hada kitabun*	هذا كتاب
This is a boy	*hada valadun*	هذا ولد
This is a house	*hada baytun*	هذا بيت
This is a business man	*hada tajirun*	هذا تاجر
This is a market	*hada sooqun*	هذا سوق
This is a pot	*hada ina'un*	هذا اناء
This is a cot	*hada sareerun*	هذا سرير
This is a shirt	*hada qameesun*	هذا قميص
This is a note book	*hada daftaru*	هذا دفتر
This is a hotel	*hada funduqun*	هذا فندق
This is a pencil	*hada mirsamun*	هذا مرسم

This is a mango	hada anbajun	هذا انبج
This is a jack fruit	hada fanasun	هذا فنس
This is a class room	hada faslun	هذا فصل
This is a lesson	hada darsun	هذا درس
This is a bucket	hada dalwun	هذا دلو
This is a lion	hada asadun	هذا أسد
This is a tiger	hada namirun	هذا نمر
This is an animal	hada haywanun	هذا حيوان
This is a guard	hada harisun	هذا حارس
This is a porter	hada shayyalun	هذا شيال
This is a manager	hada mudeerun	هذا مدير
This is a carpenter	hada najjarun	هذا نجار
This is an iron	hadihi mikvah	هذه مكواة
This is a fan	hadihi mirvaha	هذه مروحة
This is a watch	hadihi sa'a	هذه ساعة
This is a spectacle	hadihi nadara	هذه نظارة
This is a news paper	hadihi jareedah	هذه جريدة
This is a paper	hadihi varaqa	هذه ورقة
This is a washing machine	hadihi gassala	هذه غسالة
This is a car	hadihi sayyarah	هذه سيارة
This is a camel	hadihi naqah	هذه ناقة
This is a suitcase	hadihi shanta	هذه شنطة
This is a certificate	hadihi shahadah	هذه شهادة
This is a nurse	hadihi mumarrida	هذه ممرضة
This is a tree	hadihi shajarah	هذه شجرة
This is a pillow	hadihi visada	هذه وسادة
This is a stool	hadihi uskumlah	هذه اسكملة
This is a company	hadihi sharikah	هذه شركة
This is a library	hadihi makthabah	هذه مكتبة

LESSON FOUR

POSSESSIONS

In order to give our sentences strength and charm by giving accurate meaning we can use certain letters at the end of the nouns. How these letters are added and what meaning it reflect is explained here in a vivid manner.

1. If we add hu at the end of a noun we will get the meaning (his). See the examples:

This is his pen	hada qalamuhu	هذا قلمه
This is his house	hada baytuhu	هذا بيته
This is his son	hada ibnuhu	هذا ابنه

2. If we add ha at the end of a noun we will get the meaning (her). See the examples:

That is her book	dalika kitabuha	ذلك كتابها
That is her car	tilka sayyaratuha	تلك سيارتها
This is her bag	hadihi haqeebatuha	هذه حقيبتها

3. If we add huma at the end of a noun we will get the meaning (their-two). See the examples:

This is their (two) office	hada maktabuhuma	هذا مكتبهما
That is their (two) shop	dalika mahalluhuma	ذلك محلهما
That is their (two) nursery	tilka raudatuhuma	تلك روضتهما

4. If we add hum at the end of a noun we will get the meaning (their-M). See the examples:

This is their school	*hadihi madrasatuhum*	هذه مدرستهم
This is their office	*hada maktabuhum*	هذا مكتبهم
That is their teacher	*dalika mudarrisuhum*	ذلك مدرسهم

5. If we add hunna at the end of a noun we will get the meaning (their-F). See the examples:

This is their mother	*hadihi validatuhunna*	هذه والدتهن
That is their teacher	*dalika mudarrisuhunna*	ذلك مدرسهن
This is their neighbour	*hada jaruhunna*	هذا جارهن

6. If we add ka at the end of a noun we will get the meaning (your-M singular). See the examples:

This is your room	*hadihi gurfatuka*	هذه غرفتك
This is your manager	*hada mudeeruka*	هذا مديرك
This is your servant	*hada khadimuka*	هذا خادمك

7. If we add ki at the end of a noun we will get the meaning (your-F singular). See the examples:

This is your house	*hada baytuki*	هذا بيتك
That is your friend	*tilka sadeeqatuki*	تلك صديقتك
This is your friend	*hadihi zameelatuki*	هذه زميلتك

8. If we add kuma at the end of a noun we will get the meaning (your-Dual). See the examples:

That is your (two) office	*dalika maktabukuma*	ذلك مكتبكما
That is your (two) mother	*tilka ummukuma*	تلك امكما
This is your (two) son	*hada valadukuma*	هذا ولدكما

9. If we add **kum** at the end of a noun we will get the meaning (your-M. plural). See the examples:

This is your house	*hada baytukum*	هذا بيتكم
That is your shop	*dalika mahallukum*	ذلك محلكم
This is your mother	*hadihi ummukum*	هذه امكم

10. If we add **kunna** at the end of a noun we will get the meaning (your-F.plural). See the examples:

That is your park	*tilka hadeeqatukunna*	تلك حديقتكن
That is your father	*dalika validukunna*	ذلك والدكن
This is your teacher	*hada mudarrisukunna*	هذا مدرسكن

11. If we add **ee** at the end of a noun we will get the meaning (my). See the examples:

This is my house	*hada baytee*	هذا بيتي
This is my father	*hada abee*	هذا أبي
This is my mother	*hadihi ummee*	هذه أمي

12. If we add **naa** at the end of a noun we will get the meaning (our). See the examples:

This is our School	*hadihi madrasatunaa*	هذه مدرستنا
That is our company	*tilka sharikatuna*	تلك شركتنا

| That is our office | *dalika maktabuna* | ذلك مكتبنا |

We can also make our sentences effective by adding simple adjectives. See the examples:

This is an industrious boy	*hada valadun mujtahidun*	هذا ولد مجتهد
This is a big school	*hadihi madrasatun kabeeratun*	هذه مدرسة كبيرة
That is a beautiful garden	*tilka hadeeqatun jameelatun*	تلك حديقة جميلة
This is a small boy	*hada valadun sageerun*	هذا ولد صغير
That is a big man	*dalika rajulun kabeerun*	ذلك رجل كبير
This is a fat cow	*hadihi baqaratun sameenatun*	هذه بقرة سمينة
This is a famous college	*hadihi kulliyatun mash'hoorah*	هذه كلية مشهورة
That is an old university	*tilka jami'atun qadeematun*	تلك جامعة قديمة
This is a small city	*hadihi madeenatun sageeratun*	هذه مدينة صغيرة
That is a new mosque	*dalika masjidun jadeedun*	ذلك مسجد جديد
That is an old washing machine	*tilka gassalatun qadeematun*	تلك غسالة قديمة
This is a new fridge	*hadihi thallajatun jadeedatun*	هذه ثلاجة جديدة
That is a tall man	*dalika rajulun taveelun*	ذلك رجل طويل
That is a beautiful girl	*tilka bintun jameelatun*	تلك بنت جميلة

28

That is an important book	dalika kitabun muhimmun	ذلك كتاب مهم
This is an urgent message	hadihi risalatun a'jilatun	هذه رسالة عاجلة
This is a spacious shop	hada mahallun vasi'un	هذا محل واسع
That is a conjusted room	tilka gurfatun dayyikatun	تلك غرفة ضيقة
This is a small village	hadihi qar'yatun sageeratun	هذه قرية صغيرة
That is a big flat	tilka shiqatun kabeeratun	تلك شقة كبيرة
This is a small company	hadihi sharikatun sageeratun	هذه شركة صغيرة
This is a new teacher	hada mudarrissun jadeedun	هذا مدرس جديد
That is a heavy bag	dalika keesun thaqeelun	ذلك كيس ثقيل
This is an expert doctor	hadihi tabeebatun mahiratun	هذه طبيبة ماهرة
That is an old nurse	tilka mumarridatun qadeematun	تلك ممرضة قديمة

We can also make simple nominal sentences without using demonstrative pronouns. For this purpose we use al before the noun. Usually al serves the purpose of the definite article 'the' in English.

See the examples:

| The boy is big | al waladu kabeerun | الولد كبير |
| The student is sick | al talibu saqeemun | الطالب سقيم |

The reading is useful	*al qira'atu mufeedatun*	القراءة مفيدة
The cow is slim	*al baqaratu naheefatun*	البقرة نحيفة
The summer (hot) is severe	*al harru shadeedun*	الحر شديد
The ground is vast	*al mal'abu wasi'un*	الملعب واسع
The mosque is near	*al masjidu qareebun*	المسجد قريب
The house is far	*al baytu ba'eedun*	البيت بعيد
The door is open	*al babu mafthoohun*	الباب مفتوح
The office is closed	*al maktabu mu'allaqun*	المكتب مغلق
The examination is near	*al imtihanu qareebun*	الامتحان قريب
The test in tough	*al ikhtibaru sa'abun*	الاختبار صعب
The job is easy	*al shughlu sahlun*	الشغل سهل
The hotel is clean	*al funduqu nadeefun*	الفندق نظيف

SUN LETTERS AND MOON LETTERS

Arabic alphabet can be divided in to sun letters and moon letters. For a beginner to identify sun letters and moon letters we may add al before the word. If al is pronounced the letter is moon letter if not it is a sun letter.

See the examples:

bintun	بنت	al bintu	البنت
jamalun	جمل	al jamalu	الجمل
hablun	حبل	hablu	الحبل

kharoofun	خروف	al kharoofu	الخروف
dalvun	دلو	addalvu	الدلو
rizkun	رزق	arrizku	الرزق
zoujun	زوج	azzouju	الزوج

Once al is added before the Noun it will loose its nunation, because al and nunation will never come together in a word.

We can also form sentences by using possessions and adjectives together as it is explained in the following examples:

His house is big	*baytuhu kabeerun*	بيته كبير
Her car is new	*sayyaratuha jadeedatun*	سيارتها جديدة
Their office is small	*maktabuhuma sageerun*	مكتبهما صغير
Their school is near	*madrasatuhum qareebun*	مدرستهم قريبة
Their factory is old	*masna'uhunna qadeemun*	مصنعهن قديم
Your wife is beautiful	*zoujatuka jameelatun*	جميلة زوجتك
Your (two) manager is tall	*mudeerukuma taveelun*	مديركما طويل
Your field is wide	*haqlukum vasi'um*	حقلكم واسع
Your mother is a scholar	*ummukunna a'limatun*	امكن عالمة
My son is an engineer	*ibnee muhandisun*	ابني مهندس
Our teacher is sincere	*mudarrisuna mukhlisun*	مدرسنا مخلص

LESSON FIVE

PRONOUNS

While forming sentences sometimes pronouns are used instead of nouns. The most commonly used pronouns are the following:

He	*huwa*	هو
They (Two)	*huma*	هما
They	*hum*	هم
She	*hiya*	هي
They (Two)	*huma*	هما
They	*hunna*	هن
You	*anta*	انت
You (Two)	*antuma*	انتما
You	*antum*	انتم
You	*anti*	انت
You (Two)	*antuma*	انتما
You	*antunna*	انتن
I	*ana*	انا
We	*nahnu*	نحن

In Arabic nouns are classified as singular, dual and plural. Pronouns are also used in this pattern.

To change a singular noun into dual we need to add *aani* at the end of the noun when it comes as subject (in nominative case) and *ayni* when it comes as object (in accusative and ginetive cases).

For example:

A boy	*valadun*	ولد
Two boys	*valadani*	ولدان
A girl	*bintun*	بنت
Two girls	*bintani*	بنتان
A car	*sayyaratun*	سيارة
Two cars	*sayyaratani*	سيارتان
A book	*kitabun*	كتاب
Two books	*kitabaini*	كتابين
A pen	*qalamun*	قلم
Two pens	*qalamaini*	قلمين
A boy	*valadun*	ولد
Two boys	*valadaini*	ولدين
He is a teacher	*huwa mu'allimun*	هو معلم
They (two) are teachers	*huma mu'allimani*	هما معلمان
They are teachers	*hum mu'allimuna*	هم معلمون
She is a doctor	*hiya tabeebatun*	هي طبيبة
They (two) are (lady) doctors	*huma tabeebatani*	هما طبيبتان
They are (lady) doctors	*hunna tabeebaatun*	هن طبيبات
You are an engineer	*anta muhandisun*	انت مهندس

You (two) are engineers	antuma muhandisani	انتما مهندسان
You are engineers	antum muhandisoona	انتم مهندسون
You are a teacher	anti mudarrisatun	انت مدرسة
You (two) are teachers	antuma mudarrisatani	انتما مدرستان
You are teachers	antunna mudarrisaatun	انتن مدرسات
I'am a pilot	ana tayyarun	انا طيار
I'am an air hostess	ana mudeefatun	انا مضيفة
We are teachers (male)	nahnu mudarrisoona	نحن مدرسون
We are teachers (female)	nahnu mudarrisaatun	نحن مدرسات
He is famous	huwa mash'hoorun	هو مشهور
They (two male) are industrious	huma mujtahidani	هما مجتهدان
They (male) are tall	hum tiwalun	هم طوال
She is beautiful	hiya jameelatun	هي جميلة
They (two women) are beautiful	huma jameelatani	هما جميلتان
They are beautiful	hunna jameelaatun	هن جميلات
You are short	anta qaseerun	انت قصير
You (two male) are tall	antuma taveelani	انتما طويلان
You are tall	antum tivalun	انتم طوال
You (female) are new	anti jadeedatun	انت جديدة
You (two female) are new	antuma jadeedatani	انتما جديدتان

You are new	*antunna judadun*	انتن جدد
I'm strong	*ana qaviyyun*	انا قوي
We are teachers	*nahnu mudarrisoona*	نحن مدرسون
We are tall	*nahnu tivalun*	نحن طوال
He is a famous teacher	*huwa mu'allimun mash'hurun*	هو معلم مشهور
They (two) are industriou teachers	*huma mu'allimani mujtahidani*	هما معلمان مجتهدان
They are tall teachers	*hum mu'allimoona tivalun*	هم معلمون طوال
She is a beautiful doctor	*hiya tabeebatun jameelatun*	هي طبيبة جميلة
They (two) are beautiful doctors	*huma tabeebatani jameelatani*	هما طبيبتان جميلتان
They are beautiful doctors	*hunna tabeebatun jameelaatun*	هن طبيبات جميلات
You are a short engineer	*anta muhandisun qaseerun*	انت مهندس قصير
You (two) are tall engineers	*antuma muhandisani taveelani*	انتما مهندسان طويلان
You are tall engineers	*antum muhandisoona tivalun*	انتم مهندسون طوال
You (female) are a new teacher	*anti mudarrisatun jadeedatun*	انت مدرسة جديدة
You (two) are new teachers	*antuma mudarisatani jadeedatani*	انتما مدرستان جديدتان
You are new teachers	*antunna mudarrisatun judad*	انتن مدرسات جدد

I' m a new air hostess	*ana mudeefa jadeedah*	انا مضيفة جديدة
We are new teachers	*nahnu mudarrisoona judad*	نحن مدرسون جدد
We are industrious teachers	*nahnu mudarrisatun mujtahidatun*	نحن مدرسات مجتهدات

Once we practice formation of sentences in its different levels we will be thorough with reading and writing of all kinds of nominal sentences. We can also communicate simple things in Arabic.

LESSON SIX

VERBS

Like in any other language verbs play a very important role in Arabic. Verbs can be divided into past, present, imperative and prohibitive.

PAST TENSE

A verb referring to the occurrence of an action in the past is called past tense. In Arabic a past tense should have the following specifications.

1. Minimum of three letters

2. Starting and ending letter should have fatahat

3. In case of three lettered verb all letters should have a vowel (No sukoon should be there on any letter.) some examples are given below with their meaning.

To write	kataba	كتب
To sit	jalasa	جلس
To eat	akala	اكل
To beat	daraba	ضرب
To help	nasara	نصر
To go out	kharaja	خرج
To get down	nazala	نزل
To sleep	naama	نام
To wear	labisa	لبس

To stand	qaama	قام
To give up	taraka	ترك
To run	far'ra	فر
To tell truth	sadaqa	صدق
To witness	shahida	شهد
To jump	vathaba	وثب
To come	jaa'a	جاء
To come near	qaruba	قرب
To circle	daara	دار
To cut	qatha'a	قطع
To dig	hafara	حفر
To cheat	khaana	خان
To collect	jama'a	جمع
To search	bahatha	بحث
To fly	tara	طار
To enter	dakhala	دخل
To talk	hadatha	حدث
To migrate	hajara	هجر
To accept	qabila	قبل
To pull	sahaba	سحب
To carry	hamala	حمل
To permit	samaha	سمح
To understand	fahima	فهم
To see	ra'aa	رأى

To know	a'rafa	عرف
To succeed	najaha	نجح
To fail	rasaba	رسب
To drink	shariba	شرب
To slip	zalaqa	زلق
To hit	ta'ana	طعن
To throw	ramaa	رمى
To cover	satara	ستر
To ask	talaba	طلب
To swim	sabaha	سبح
To return	a'ada	عاد
To be away	ba'uda	بعد
To separate	fasala	فصل
To exhaust	tha'iba	تعب
To warn	nadara	نذر
To memorise	hafida	حفظ
To profit	rabiha	ربح
To get angry	gadiba	غضب
To win	faaza	فاز
To stay	sakana	سكن
To meet	laqiya	لقي
To type/print	taba'a	طبع
To enter	salaka	سلك
To publish	nashara	نشر

To follow	tabi'a	تبع
To pour	sabba	صب
To rise	rafa'a	رفع
To sell	baa'a	باع
To pluck	qatafa	قطف
To study	darasa	درس
To go	dahaba	ذهب
To read	qara'a	قرأ
To look	nadara	نظر
To open	fataha	فتح
To ride	rakiba	ركب
To elevate	sa'ida	صعد
To wake up	nahada	نهض
To wash	gasala	غسل
To feed	razaqa	رزق
To take	akhada	أخذ
To divide	qasama	قسم
To lie	kadaba	كذب
To promise	va'ada	وعد
To stand	vaqafa	وقف
To sweep	kanasa	كنس
To say	qaala	قال
To hold	qabada	قبض
To burn	haraqa	حرق

To draw	*rasama*	رسم
To calculate	*hasiba*	حسب
To dance	*raqasa*	رقص
To prevent	*mana'a*	منع
To fall	*vaqa'a*	وقع
To impose	*farada*	فرض
To jail	*sajana*	سجن
To refuse	*rafada*	رفض
To pay	*dafa'a*	دفع
To permit	*adina*	أذن
To hear	*sami'a*	سمع
To find	*vajada*	وجد
To kow	*alima*	علم
To appear	*dahara*	ظهر
To escape	*salima*	سلم
To love	*habba*	حب
To snatch	*khatafa*	خطف
To ring	*daq'qa*	دق
To nominate	*rashaha*	رشح
To delete	*hadafa*	حذف
To play	*la'iba*	لعب
To return	*raja'a*	رجع
To come near	*danaa*	دنا
To seperate	*faraqa*	فرق

To thirst	*a'tasha*	عطش
To prescribe	*vasafa*	وصف
To be able	*qadara*	قدر
To be happy	*fariha*	فرح
To rub	*masaha*	مسح
To ask	*sa'ala*	سأل
To fall	*saqata*	سقط
To call / to invite	*da'aa*	دعا
To cook	*tabakha*	طبخ
To weave	*nasaja*	نسج
To solve	*halla*	حل
To support	*da'ama*	دعم
To rule	*hakama*	حكم
To complain	*shakaa*	شكا
To cry	*bakaa*	بكى
To smile	*basama*	بسم

If we add ma before a past tense we will get negative meening.

For example:

He wrote	*kataba*	كتب
He didn't write	*ma kataba*	ما كتب
He went	*dahaba*	ذهب
He did not go	*ma dahaba*	ما ذهب
He helped	*nasara*	نصر

42

He did not help	ma nasara	ما نصر
He opened	fataha	فتح
He did not open	ma fataha	ما فتح
He ate	akala	أكل
He did not eat	ma akala	ما أكل

In Arabic communication is made in the most effective way by using accurate forms of the verb. For this purpose we can make fourteen steps from any given verb. The process of making 14 steps from a given verb is called conjugation in Arabic grammar. How this is done in a past tense is shown below. If you are thorough with one verb you can make any verb in the same format. Fourteen steps from kataba is given as an example.

He wrote	kataba	كتب
They (Two men) wrote	katabaa	كتبا
They wrote	kataboo	كتبوا
She wrote	katabat	كتبت
They (Two men) wrote	katabataa	كتبتا
They wrote	katabna	كتبن
You (a male) wrote	katabta	كتبت
You (Two male) wrote	katabtuma	كتبتما
You (M) wrote	katabtum	كتبتم
You (F) wrote	katabti	كتبت
You (two F) wrote	katabtuma	كتبتما
You (F) wrote	katabtunna	كتبتن
I wrote	katabtu	كتبت
We wrote	katbnaa	كتبنا

PRESENT TENSE

To make a past tense into present tense we have to follow the steps.

1. Add a / ta/ ya/ na in the beginning of the past tense. This is based on the subject. If I come as subject add a, if the subject is we, add na, If the subject is he or they add ya and if the subject is you or she add ta. In this way by simply looking at the beginning of a present tense we will get clear clues regarding the subject.

2. Remove the symbol of the first basic letter and give sukoon.

3. Put Dammah to the last letter.

Some examples are given to convince you how this is made:

He opened	*fataha*	فتح
He opens	*yaftahu*	يفتح
He wrote	*kataba*	كتب
He writes	*yaktubu*	يكتب
He knew	*alima*	علم
He knows	*ya'lamu*	يعلم
He beat	*daraba*	ضرب
He beats	*yadribu*	يضرب

We can also make 14 steps from a given present tense. See the example:

He writes	*yaktubu*	يكتب
They (2 M) write	*yaktubani*	يكتبان
They write	*yaktuboona*	يكتبون
She writes	*taktubu*	تكتب

They (2 F) write	*taktubaani*	تكتبان
They write	*yaktubna*	يكتبن
You write	*taktubu*	تكتب
You (2 F) write	*taktubaani*	تكتبان
You write	*taktuboona*	تكتبون
You (F) write	*taktubeena*	تكتبين
You (2 F) write	*taktubaani*	تكتبان
You write	*taktubna*	تكتبن
I write	*aktubu*	أكتب
We write	*naktubu*	نكتب

If we put la before a present tense we will get the negative meaning. For eg if we say la yaktubu it means he is not writing.

He writes	*yaktubu*	يكتب
He does not write	*la yaktubu*	لا يكتب
He goes	*yadhabu*	يذهب
He does not go	*la yadhabu*	لا يذهب
He helps	*yansuru*	ينصر
He does not help	*la yansuru*	لا ينصر

It is highly recommended that each learner should posses a number of verbs of their choice to make verbal sentences according to the situations.

While forming verbal sentences the preferable pattern is Verb, Subject, Object (VSO)

TRANSITIVE AND INTRANSITIVE VERBS

Verbs can be divided into transitive and intransitive verbs. Verbs having object is called Transitive verbs.

Examples:

The boy wrote the lesson	*katabal valadu addarsa*	كتب الولد الدرس
The boy did not write the lesson	*ma katabal valadu addarsa*	ما كتب الولد الدرس
The boy writes the lesson	*yaktubul valadu addarsa*	يكتب الولد الدرس
The boy does not write the lesson	*la yaktubul valadu addarsa*	لا يكتب الولد الدرس
The servant opened the door	*fatahal khadimu al baba*	فتح الخادم الباب
The servant did not open the door	*ma fatahal khadimu al baba*	ما فتح الخادم الباب
The servant opens the door	*yaftahul khadimu al baba*	يفتح الخادم الباب
The servant does not open the door	*la yaftahul khadimu al baba*	لا يفتح الخادم الباب
The rich helped the poor	*nasaral ganiyyu al faqeera*	نصر الغني الفقير
The rich did not help the poor	*ma nasaral ganiyyu al faqeera*	ما نصر الغني الفقير
The rich helps the poor	*yansurul ganiyyu al faqeera*	ينصر الغني الفقير
The rich does not help the poor	*la yansurun ganiyyu al faqeera*	لا ينصر الغني الفقير

46

Verbs not having object is called intransitive verbs.
Examples:

The boy laughed	*dahikal valadu*	ضحك الولد
The boy did not laugh	*ma dahikal valadu*	ما ضحك الولد
The boy laughs	*yadhakul valadu*	يضحك الولد
The boy does not laugh	*la yadhakul valadu*	لا يضحك الود
The crow flew	*taaral gurabu*	طار الغراب
The crow did not fly	*ma taaral gurabu*	ما طار الغراب
The crow flies	*yateerul gurabu*	يطير الغراب
The crow does not fly	*la yateerul gurabu*	لا يطير الغراب
The lion slept	*naamal asadu*	نام الأسد
The lion did not sleep	*ma naamal asadu*	ما نام الأسد
The lion sleeps	*yanaamul asadu*	ينام الأسد
The lion does not sleep	*la yanaamul asadu*	لا ينام الأسد

IMPERATIVE VERBS

Imperative verbs are formed from the Present tense. To make imperative verb from the third person we need to bring li in the beginning and put jussive case at the end.

See the examples given:

yaktubu	يكتب	Yajlisu	يجلس	Yansuru	ينصر
liyaktub	ليكتب	liyajlis	ليجلس	liyansur	لينصر
liyaktubaa	ليكتبا	liyajlisaa	ليجلسا	liyansuraa	لينصرا
liyaktuboo	ليكتبوا	liyajlisoo	ليجلسوا	liyansuroo	لينصروا
litaktub	لتكتب	Litajlis	لتجلس	litansur	لتنصر

litaktubaa	لتكتبا	litajlisaa	لتجلسا	litansuraa	لتنصرا
liyaktubna	ليكتبن	liyajlisna	ليجلسن	liyansurna	لينصرن

How imperative verbs are formed form the second person is explained in the following examples:

Kataba	كتب	jalasa	جلس	vaqafa	وقف
yaktubu	يكتب	yajlisu	يجلس	yaqifu	يقف
Uktub	أكتب	ijlis	اجلس	qif	قف
uktubaa	أكتبا	ijlisa	اجلسا	qifa	قفا
uktoboo	أكتبوا	ijlisoo	اجلسوا	qifoo	قفوا
uktubaa	أكتبا	ijlisaa	اجلسا	qifaa	قفا
uktubee	أكتبي	ijlisee	اجلسي	qifee	قفي
uktubaa	أكتبا	ijlisaa	اجلسا	qifa	قفا
uktubna	أكتبن	ijlisna	اجلسن	qifna	قفن

PROHIBITIVE COMMAND

Prohibitive command is also made from the present tense. To get this we need to put la before a present tense and make jussive case at the end.

Examples:

tadhabu	تذهب	taktubu	تكتب	tansuru	تنصر
la tadhab	لا تذهب	la taktub	لا تكتب	la tansur	لا تنصر

la tadhaba لا تذهبا	la taktubaa لا تكتبا	la tansuraa لا تنصرا
la tadhaboo لا تذهبوا	la taktuboo لا تكتبوا	la tansuroo لا تنصروا
la tadhabee لا تذهبي	la taktubee لا تكتبي	la tansuree لا تنصري
la tadhabaa لا تذهبا	la taktubaa لا تكتبا	la tansuraa لا تنصرا
la tadhabna لا تذهبن	la taktubna لا تكتبن	la tansurna لا تنصرن

LESSON SEVEN

PREPOSITIONS

Very often we need prepositions to form effective structures of communication. I would like to introduce here some commonly used prepositions.

1. FROM (MIN) من

Examples:

The boy returned from the school	*raja'al valadu minal madrasati*	رجع الولد من المدرسة
Mohammed went out from home	*kharaja muhammadun minal bayti*	خرج محمد من البيت
He is from India	*huwa minal hindi*	هو من الهند

2. TO (ILA) إلى

Examples:

My father went to the market	*dahaba abee ilassooqi*	ذهب أبي الى السوق
The student goes to the school	*yadhabu taalibu ilal madrasati*	يذهب الطالب الى المدرسة
The boy wrote a letter to his father	*katabal valadu risala ila abeehi*	كتب الولد رسالة الى ابيه

3. ABOUT ('AN) عن

The teacher asked about Mohammed	*sa'alal mudarrisu 'an muhammadin*	سأل المدرس عن محمد

| The students discussed about the vacation | naqashatullabu 'anil ijaza | ناقش الطلاب عن الاجازة |
| The manager spoke about the business | kallamal mudeeru 'anitijarati | كلم المدير عن التجارة |

4. ON (‘ALA) على

The boy sat on the bench	jalasal valadu 'alal mak'adi	جلس الولد على المقعد
The teacher wrote on the board	katabal mu'allimu 'alassabboorati	كتب المعلم على السبورة
There is a crow on the tree	alashajarati gurabun	على الشجرة غراب

5. IN (FEE) في

The manager slept in the office	naamal mudeeru fil maktabi	نام المدير في المكتب
The pen is in the pocket	al qalamu fil jaybi	القلم في الجيب
The doctor is in the hospital	atabeebu fil mustashfa	الطبيب في المستشفى

6. WITH (BI) بِ

I wrote with the pen	katabtu bil qalami	كتبت بالقلم
The boy played with the ball	la'ibalvaladu bil kurathi	لعب الولد بالكرة
The butcher slew the goat with the knife	dabahal jazzaru ashshata bissikkeeni	ذبح الجزار الشاة بالسكين

51

7. FOR (LI) لِ

The elephant has a trunk	lil feeli khurtoomun	للفيل خرطوم
This is for me	hada lee	هذا لي
The manager has a car	lil mudeeri sayyaratun	للمدير سيارة

8. WITH (M'A) مع

The teacher went with the principal	dahabal mudarrisu ma'al mudeeri	ذهب المدرس مع المدير
Mohammed walked with his wife	mashaa mohammedun ma'a zaujatihi	مشى محمد مع زوجته
The child slept with his mother	naamatiflu ma'a ummihi	نام الطفل مع أمه
With him	ma'ahu	معه
With them(Dual)	ma'humaa	معهما
with them (plural-M)	ma'hum	معهم
With her	ha'ahaa	معها
With them (plural-F)	ma'ahunna	معهن
With you	ma'aka	معك
With you (Dual)	ma'akumaa	معكما
With you (plural-M)	ma'akum	معكم
With you	ma'aki	معك

With you (plural)	ma'akunna	معكن
With me	ma'ee	معي
With us	ma'anaa	معنا

9.   ABOVE   (FOUQA)   فوق

The crow flew above the tree	taaral gurabu fouqashshajarati	طار الغراب فوق الشجرة
The aeroplane flew above the mountain	taarathi taa'iratu fouqal jabali	طارت الطائرة فوق الجبل
There is a tree above my house	fouqa baytee shajaratun	فوق بيتي شجرة

10.   UNDER   (TAHTA)   تحت

The boy played under the tree	la'ibal valadu tahta shshajarati	لعب الولد تحت الشجرة
My flat is under the flat of the principal	shiqatee tahta shiqatil mudeeri	شقتي تحت شقة المدير
The paradise is under the feet of mothers	al jannatu tahta aqdamil ummahat	الجنة تحت اقدام الأمهات

11.   BEFORE   (QABLA)   قبل

I took bath before food	gasaltu qablal akli	غسلت قبل الاكل
I thought before talking	fakartu qablal kalami	فكرت قبل الكلام
I understood the lesson before the examination	fahimtuddarsa qablal imtihani	فهمت الدرس قبل الامتحان

12.　　AFTER　　(BA'DA)　بعد

I returned from the school after Asr	*raja'tu minal madrasati ba'dal asri*	رجعت من المدرسة بعد العصر
The wage is after work	*al ajru ba'dal 'amal*	الأجر بعد العمل
The boy wrote after reading	*katabal valadu ba'dal qira'ati*	كتب الولد بعد القراءة

13.　　BETWEEN (BAYNA)　بين

The teacher stood between the table and chair	*qamal mudarrisu byna taavilati val kursiyyi*	قام المدرس بين الطاولة والكرسي
There is a river between the school and the mosque	*baynal madrasati val masjidi nahrun*	بين المدرسة والمسجد نهر
The boy played between Asr and Magrib	*laibal valadu baynal asri wal magribi*	لعب الولد بين العصر والمغرب

14.　　HAS/HAVE　(ÍNDA)　عند

inda can be used in different meanings. The most common usage is for has and have. But in some cases it is used for the meaning near.

Examples will further clarify this point.

| The driver is near the Manager | *a'ssaiqu índal Mudeer* | السائق عند المدير |
| The calf is near the cow | *al ijli índal baqarati* | العجل عند البقرة |

54

The student has a bag	*índa taalibi haqeebatun*	عند الطالب حقيبة
He has a car	*índahu sayyaratun*	عنده سيارة
They have books	*índahuma kutubun*	عندهما كتب
They have money	*índahum fuloosun*	عندهم فلوس
She has a cycle	*índaha darrajah*	عندها دراجة
They have pens	*índahunna aqlamun*	عندهن اقلام
You have a cow	*índaka baqaratun*	عندك بقرة
You have a servant	*índakuma khadimun*	عندكما خادم
You have job	*Índakum shuglun*	عندكم شغل
You have a bag	*índaki haqeebah*	عندك حقيبة
You have a maid	*índakunna khadimah*	عندكن خادمة
I have 100 dollars	*índee miatu doolarun*	عندي ١٠٠ دولار
We have a car	*índanaa sayyarah*	عندنا سيارة

LESSON EIGHT

DAY/ WEEK/ MONTH/ YEAR

A day	*yaumun*	يوم
Today (the day)	*alyaumu*	اليوم
Yesterday	*Ams*	أمس
Day before yesterday	*awwal ams*	أول أمس
Tomorrow	*bukra*	بكرة
Tomorrow	*gad*	غد
Day after tomorrow	*ba'da bukra*	بعد بكرة
An hour	*saaá*	ساعة
Half an hour	*niswfu ssaaá*	نصف ساعة
A quarter	*rubú ssaaá*	ربع ساعة
A minute	*daqeeqa*	دقيقة
A second	*thaniya*	ثانية
Night	*layl*	ليل
Day	*nahar*	نهار
Week	*usbooe*	أسبوع
Days of the week	***ayyamul usboo'***	أيام الأسبوع
Sunday	*yaumul ahad*	يوم الأحد
Monday	*yaumul ithnayn*	يوم الاثنين
Tuesday	*yaumu thulathae*	يوم الثلاثاء

DAY / WEEK / MONTH / YEAR

Wednesday	yaumul árbiae	يوم الأربعاء
Thursday	yaumul khamees	يوم الخميس
Friday	yaumul Jumuá	يوم الجمعة
Saturday	yaumussabt	يوم السبت
A month	shahrun	شهر
A year	sanah / ám	سنة / عام
Date	tareekh	تاريخ

LESSON NINE

PARTS OF THE BODY

Head	*ra'sun*	رأس
Hair	*sha'run*	شعر
Fore-head	*jabeen*	جبين
Face	*vajhun*	وجه
Cheek	*khadd*	خد
Eye	*áyn*	عين
Ear	*udn*	أذن
Nose	*anf*	أنف
Mouth	*fam*	فم
Lip	*shafath*	شفة
Tongue	*lisan*	لسان
Teeth	*sinn*	سن
Mustouche	*shavarib*	شوارب
Beard	*lihya*	لحية
Throat	*halq*	حلق
Shoulder	*únuq*	عنق
Back	*dahr*	ظهر
Chest	*sadr*	صدر

Heart	*qalb*	قلب
Hand	*yad*	يد
Stomack	*batn*	بطن
Thigh	*fakhdh*	فخذ
Knee	*rukba*	ركبة
Leg	*rijl*	رجل
Foot	*qadam*	قدم

LESSON TEN
PROFESSIONS

Accountant	*muhasib*	محاسب
Air hostess	*muzeefah*	مضيفة
Attender	*jarsoon*	جرسون
Ayah	*murabbiya*	مربية
Banker	*swairafee*	صيرفي
Black smith	*haddad*	حداد
Broker	*simsar*	سمسار
Butcher	*lahham*	لحام
Carpenter	*najjar*	نجار
Cashier	*ameenu ssundooq*	أمين الصندوق
Clerk	*katib*	كاتب
Cobbler	*saqqaf*	سقاف
Contractor	*muqavil*	مقاول
Cook	*tabbakh*	طباخ
Doctor	*daktoor*	دكتور
Doctor	*tabeeb*	طبيب
Artist / draftsman	*rassam*	رسام
Driver	*saaiq*	سائق

Editor	muharrir	محرر
Electrician	kahrbaee	كهربائي
Engineer	muhandis	مهندس
Fisherman	sammak	سماك
Guard	haris	حارس
Inspector	mufatish	مفتش
Lawyer	muhami	محامي
Librarian	ameenul maktaba	أمين المكتبة
Manager	mudeer	مدير
Principal	mudeer	مدير
Mason	bannae	بناء
Office boy	farrash	فراش
Pharmacist	saidalee	صيدلى
Scientist	áalim	عالم
Supervisor	mushrif	مشرف
Pilot	tayyar	طيار
Police	shurtee	شرطي
Porter	shayyal	شيال
Salesman	baeh	بائع
Surveyor	massah	مساح
Tailor	khayat	خياط
Teacher	mudarris	مدرس
Teacher	muállim	معلم

Operator	*mushagil*	مشغل
Translator	*mutarjim*	مترجم
Agent	*wakeel*	وكيل
Helper	*musaid*	مساعد
Researcher	*bahith*	باحث
Nurse	*mumarrid*	ممرض
Guide	*murshid*	مرشد
Observer / censor	*muraqib*	مراقب
Farmer	*muzarie*	مزارع
Headmaster	*nadir*	ناظر
Headmistress	*nadirah*	ناظرة
Lab technician	*fannee mukhtabar*	فني مختبر
Telephone operator	*mushagil telephone*	مشغل التلفون
TV operator	*mushagil talfiziyoon*	مشغل التلفزيون

LESSON ELEVEN

SOME USEFUL WORDS

Yes	*ayva*	أيوا
Yes	*eee*	اي
No	*mush*	مش
No	*mub*	مب
No	*moo*	مو
This is not nice	*hada mub ẓayn*	هذا مب زين
This is not nice	*hada moo ẓayn*	هذا مو زين
Not this	*mush hada*	مش هذا
Yes	*naám*	نعم
No	*laa*	لا
Please	*min fadlik*	من فضلك
If you don't mind	*law samahta*	لو سمحت
Thanks	*shukran*	شكرا
Thanks	*mashkoor*	مشكور
Excuse me	*áfvan*	عفوا
Congrats	*mabrook*	مبروك
Sorry	*ásif*	آسف
No	*laysa*	ليس

Available	*moujood*	موجود
Exchange	*thahveelah*	تحويلة
Excuse me	*samihnee*	سامحني
Passport	*javvazu ssafar*	جواز السفر
Visa	*ta'sheerah*	تأشيرة
Visit visa	*ta'esheerah ziyarah*	تأشيرة زيارة
Employment visa	*ta'esheerah ámal*	تأشيرة عمل
Tourist visa	*ta'esheerah siyahah*	تأشيرة سياحة
Transit visa	*ta'esheera úboor*	تأشيرة عبور
Family visa	*ta'esheera áiliyya*	تأشيرة عائلية
Work visit	*ziyyara ámal*	زيارة عمل
Residence permit (RP)	*iqama*	إقامة
Renewal of RP	*tajdeedul iqama*	تجديد الاقامة
Validity	*salahiyyah*	صلاحية
Rate	*si'r*	سعر
Also	*aydan*	أيضا
Cancelled	*mulga*	ملغى
But	*lakin*	لكن
Trip	*rihla*	رحلة
Never	*abadan*	أبدا
Transfer of sponsorship	*naqlu kafalah*	نقل كفالة
Perhaps	*rubbama*	ربما
Release	*tanazil*	تنازل

SOME USEFUL WORDS

Contract	*áqd*	عقد
Signature	*touqee'*	توقيع
Seal	*khatm*	ختم
Permit	*tasreeh*	تصريح
License	*rukhsah*	رخصة
Temporary	*muáqat*	مؤقت
Early	*mubakkir*	مبكر
Late	*muthaákhir*	متأخر
Purpose	*garad*	غرض
Nationality	*jinsiyyah*	جنسية
Sex	*jins*	جنس
Commercial registration	*sijilli ttijari*	سجل التجارى
Rent	*eejar*	إيجار
Municipality	*baladiyya*	بلدية
Like	*mithla*	مثل
Since	*mundu*	منذ
Card	*bataqa*	بطاقة
ID card	*bataqa shakhsiyya*	بطاقة الشخصية
Health card	*bathaqatu ssihha*	بطاقة الصحة
Guarantee card	*bataqathu ddaman*	بطاقة الضمان
Insurance	*ta'meen*	تأمين
Busy	*mashgool*	مشغول

Free	fadee	فاضى
Directory	daleel	دليل
Only	faqat	فقط
Till	hatta	حتى
Without	bidoona	بدون
Commission	ámoola	عمولة
Client	zaboon	زبون
Receipt	eesal	إيصال
Invoice	fatoora	فاتورة
Loss	khasarah	خسارة
Fund	raseed	رصيد
Loan	qarad	قرض
Budget	meezaniyya	ميزانية
Debt	dein	دين
Account	hisab	حساب
Monopoly	ihtikar	إحتكار
Export	sadirat	صادرات
Import	varidat	واردات
Tax	darbiyya	ضربية
Charge/fee	rusoom	رسوم
Cash	naqd	نقد
Discount	tanzeelat	تنزيلات
Demand	talab	طلب
Production	intaj	إنتاج

SOME USEFUL WORDS

Share	*sahm*	سهم
Address	*unvan*	عنوان
Telephone	*hatif*	هاتف
Local call	*mukaalama mahalliyya*	مكالمة محلية
International call	*mukaalama kharijiyya*	مكالمة خارجية
Receiver	*samaá*	سماعة
Agency	*vakalah*	وكالة
Partner	*shareek*	شريك
Price	*thaman*	ثمن
Value	*qeemah*	قيمة
Shop	*dukkan*	دكان
Model	*namoodaj*	نموذج
Bread	*khubuz*	خبز
Juice	*áseer*	عصير
Soup	*shurbah*	شربة
Salad	*salat*	سلت
Vegetable	*khudar*	خضر
Meet / beaf	*lah'm*	لحم
Chicken	*dajaj*	دجاج
Goat	*kharoof*	خروف
Buffello	*jaamoos*	جاموس
Rabbit	*arnab*	أرنب

LESSON TWELVE

COLOURS

White	abyad	أبيض
Black	asvad	أسود
Red	ahmar	أحمر
Green	akhdar	أخضر
Blue	azraq	أزرق
Yellow	asfar	أصفر
Pink	vardee	وردي
Grey	ramadee	رمادي
Orange	burtuqalee	برتقالي
Violet	banafsajee	بنفسجي
Silver	fiddee	فضي
Golden	dahabee	ذهبي

LESSON THIRTEEN

NUMBERS

Zero	*sifr*	صفر	٠
One	*wahid*	واحد	١
Two	*ithnani*	إثنان	٢
Three	*thalatha*	ثلاثة	٣
Four	*arbaá*	أربعة	٤
Five	*khamsah*	خمسة	٥
Six	*sitta*	ستة	٦
Seven	*sabá*	سبعة	٧
Eight	*thamaniya*	ثمانية	٨
Nine	*tisá*	تسعة	٩
Ten	*áshrah*	عشرة	١٠
Eleven	*ahada ashara*	احد عشر	١١
Twelve	*itna ashara*	إثنا عشر	١٢
Thirteen	*thalatha ashara*	ثلاثة عشر	١٣
Fourteen	*arbaátha áshara*	أربعة عشر	١٤
Fifteen	*khamsata áshara*	خمسة عشر	١٥
Sixteen	*sittata áshara*	ستة عشر	١٦
Seventeen	*sabáta áshara*	سبعة عشر	١٧

Eighteen	*thamaniata áshara*	ثمانية عشر	١٨
Nineteen	*tisáta áshrah*	تسعة عشر	١٩
Twenty	*íshroon*	عشرون	٢٠
Thirty	*thalathoon*	ثلاثون	٣٠
Forty	*arbaóon*	أربعون	٤٠
Fifty	*khamsoon*	خمسون	٥٠
Sixty	*sittoon*	ستون	٦٠
Seventy	*saboon*	سبعون	٧٠
Eighty	*thamanoon*	ثمانون	٨٠
Ninety	*thisóon*	تسعون	٩٠
One hundred	*miá*	مائة	١٠٠
Two hundred	*miátaani*	مائتان	٢٠٠
Two hundred	*miátaini*	مائتين	٣٠٠
Five hundred	*khamsa miá*	خمس مائة	٥٠٠
One thousand	*alf*	ألف	١٠٠٠

Once we are able to idenify the numbers we can write any number in Arabic. Numbers are written in the same order of English and the difference will be only in reading.

See the examples:

1987	١٩٨٧
2004	٢٠٠٤
1969	١٩٦٩
1526	١٥٢٦
2845	٢٨٤٥

2836	٢٨٣٦
7128	٧١٢٨
3647	٣٦٤٧
786	٧٨٦
6236	٦٢٣٦

But the dates are written in a different way. See the examples:

30-05-1969	١٩٦٩ / ٠٥ / ٣٠
01-09-2004	٢٠٠٤ / ٩ / ١
02-05-1988	١٩٨٨ / ٥ / ٢
07-08-1986	١٩٨٦ / ٨ / ٧
05-04-1827	١٨٢٧ / ٤ / ٥

Full	kaamil	كامل
Half	nisf	نصف
Quarter	rubue	ربع
One third	thuluth	ثلث
Percent	fil miá	في المائة
All	kull	كل
Part	juzu	جزء

LESSON FOURTEEN

GREETINGS

Peace be upon you	*Assalamu alaikkum*	السلام عليكم
Peace be upon you too	*Wa alaikkumussalam*	وعليكم السلام
Good morning	*sabahal khair*	صباح الخير
Good morning (reply)	*sabahannor*	صباح النور
Good evening	*masaúl khair*	مساء الخير
Good evening (reply)	*masaúnnoor*	مساء النور
Welcome	*marhaba*	مرحبا
Welcome	*marhabatain*	مرحبتين
Hello (welcome)	*ahlan*	أهلا
Most welcome	*ahlan va sahlan*	أهلا وسهلا
Good night	*layla saéeda*	ليلة سعيدة
Glad to see you	*saéedun biliqaík*	سعيد بلقائك
Happy journey	*rihla saéeda*	رحلة سعيدة
Good bye	*ma'ssalama*	مع السلامة
Good bye	*fee amanillah*	في أمان الله

See you	*ila lliqa*	إلى اللقاء
May Allah bless you	*barakallahu feeka*	بارك الله فيك
May Allah save you	*Allah khalleek*	الله خليك
May Allah save you	*Allah yusallimaka*	الله يسلمك
May Allah be merciful on your parents	*Allah yarham validaika*	الله يرحم والديك
May Allah save you	*Allah yahfizuk*	الله يحفظك
We wish you all the best	*natamanna laka kullal khair*	نتمنى لك كل الخير
We wish you good health	*natamanna laka ssihha val áfia*	نتمنى لك الصحة والعافية
May Allah cure you	*Allahu yashfeeka*	الله يشفيك
Allah is great	*Allah kareem*	الله كريم
May Allah be pleased with you	*Allah yarda álaika*	الله يرضى عليك
May Allah reward you nicely	*jazakkallah khairan*	جزاك الله خيرا
May Allah accept	*taqabbalallah*	تقبل الله
Please come	*tafaddal*	تفضل
Please take your seat	*istarih*	إسترح
New year greetings	*kulla ámin va antun bi khair*	كل عام وانتم بخير
New Year greetings (reply)	*kulla sanah tayyib*	كل سنة طيب

73

Eid greeting	*éedukum Mubarak*	عيدكم مبارك
Good wishes	*tasbah ála khair*	تصبح على خير
Good wishes (reply)	*va anta min ahlil khair*	وانت من اهل الخير

LESSON FIFTEEN

DISEASES

Diseases	amraz	أمراض
Anemia	faqru dam	فقر دم
Cancer	sartan	سرطان
Cold	zukam	زكام
Constipation	imsak	إمساك
Cough	sual	سعال
Diarrhea	ishal	إسهال
Fever	humma	حمى
Head ache	alamu rraes/sudae	الم الرأس / الصداع
Measles	hisba	حصبة
Poisoning	tasammum	تسمم
Small pox	judree	جدري
Stomach pain	alamul batan	الم البطن
Tooth ache	alamussinn	الم السن
Tuberculosis	sall	سل
0Ulcer	qurhah	قرحة

LESSON SIXTEEN

INTERROGATIVE WORDS

I. What   شو / شن / ايش / ما

Now we come to the most important part of the course. That is Introduction of Interrogatives. If we are thorough with interrogatives and their applications, we can make any number of questions. If we ask the question, the listener will say the answer and communication can be continued.

What is your name?	*shusmuka*	شسمك
What is his name?	*shusmuhu*	شسمه
What is her name?	*shusmuhaa*	شسمها
What is the name of your school?	*shusmu madrasatika*	شسم مدرستك
What is the name of your city?	*shusmu madeenatika*	شسم مدينتك
What is the name of your teacher?	*shusmu mudarrisika*	شسم مدرسك
What is the name of your classmate?	*shusmu zameelika*	شسم زميلك
What is the name of your manager?	*shusmu mudeerika*	شسم مديرك
What is the name of your father?	*shusmu abeeka*	شسم أبيك
What is the name of your mother?	*shusmu ummika*	شسم أمك

What is the name of your husband?	*shusmu zoujiki*	شسم زوجك
What is the name of your wife?	*shusmu zoujatika*	شسم زوجتك
What is the name of your company?	*shusmu sharikatika*	شسم شركتك
What is the name of your house?	*shusmu baytika*	شسم بيتك
What is the name of your partner?	*shusmu sharekuka*	شسم شريكك
What is the name of your neighbour?	*shusmu jaruka*	شسم جارك
What is the name of your doctor?	*shusmu tabeebika*	شسم طبيبك
What is the name of your shop?	*shusmu mahallika*	شسم محلك
What is the name of your brother?	*shusmu akheeka*	شسم أخيك
What is the name of your sister?	*shusmu ukhthika*	شسم أختك
What is the name of your son?	*shusmi ibnika*	شسم إبنك
What is the name of your daughter?	*shusmu ibnatika*	شسم إبنتك
What is the name of your sponsor?	*shusmu kafeelika*	شسم كفيلك
What is this	*shoo hada*	شو هذا

What is this	*sho hadihee*	شو هذه
What is the problem	*esh fee*	ايش فيه
What is the problem	*shunu fee*	شن فيه
What is the problem	*shunu fee mushkila*	شن في مشكلة
What is the problem (difficulty)	*shunul mashaqa*	شن المشقة
What you want	*shunu tabgee*	شن تبغ
What you want	*shunu tureedu*	شن تريد
What you want	*esh tabgee*	ايش تبغ
What you want	*esh tureedu*	ايش تريد
What is the solution?	*shunul hall*	شن الحل
What is the suggetion?	*shunul iqtirah*	شن الاقتراح
What is the result	*shunu nnateejah*	شن النتيجة
What do you do there	*shusavvee hinaka*	شو سوى هناك
What do you drink	*shunu tashrab*	شن تشرب
What would you like to drink	*tuhib tashrab esh*	تحب تشرب ايش
What would you like to eat	*tuhib ta'kula esh*	تحب تأكل ايش
What would you like to wear?	*tuhibb talbas esh*	تحب تلبس ايش
What would you like to write?	*tuhibb ta'ktuba esh*	تحب تكتب ايش
What would you like to talk	*tuhibb tuhaddatha esh*	تحب تحدث ايش

78

What he says?	*shunu yaqool*	شن يقول
What he says?	*esh yaqool*	ايش يقول
What did I tell you?	*aqullaka esh*	أقلك ايش
What do they call it in Arabic?	*shoo sammoona hada bil árabee*	شو سمون هذا بالعربي؟
What do they call it in English?	*shoo sammoona hada bin injleesi*	شو سمون هذا بالانجليزي؟
What does it mean?	*shoo ya'nee*	شو يعني

II. Where   *ayna / vaina*   وين / أين

Where are you?	*vayn inta*	وين إنت
Where are you?	*vaynaka*	وينك
Where are you from?	*min vayna inta*	من وين إنت
Where is he from?	*min vayna huwa*	من وين هو
Where is she from?	*min vayn hiya*	من وين هي
Where is your house?	*vayn baytuka*	وين بيتك
Where is your school?	*vain madrasatuka*	وين مدرستك
Where is your Office?	*vain maktabuka*	وين مكتبك
Where is your father?	*vain abooka*	وين أبوك
Where is your mother	*vain ummuka*	وين أمك
Where is your husband?	*vain zoujuka*	وين زوجك
Where is your wife?	*vain zoujatuka*	وين زوجتك
Where is your brother?	*vain akhooka*	وين أخوك
Where is your sister?	*vain ukhtuka*	وين أختك

79

Where are you going?	*vain rooh*	وين رح
Where are you going?	*vain taruh*	وين ترح
Where do you work?	*vain tashtagil*	وين تشتغل
Where do you sleep?	*vain tanaam*	وين تنام
Where do you play?	*vain tal'ab*	وين تلعب
Where do you take rest?	*vain tartah*	وين ترتاح

Where can I find?	***vain ajid***	وين أجد
Where can I find a hotel?	*vain ajid funduqun*	وين أجد فندقا
Where can I find a school?	*vain ajid madrasah*	وين أجد مدرسة
Where can I find a hospital?	*vain ajid mustashfa*	وين أجد مستشفى
Where can I find a bank?	*vain ajid masrafan*	وين أجد مصرفا
Where can I find a servant?	*vain ajid khadiman*	وين أجد خادما
Where can I find a driver?	*vain ajid sa'eqan*	وين أجد سائقا
Where can I find an interpreter?	*vain ajid mutarjiman*	وين أجد مترجما
Where can I find a mosque?	*vain ajid masjidan*	وين أجد مسجدا
Where can I find a toilet?	*vain ajid hammaman*	وين أجد حماما

80

Where can I find a helper?	*vain ajid musa'idan*	وين أجد مساعدا
Where can I find an engineer?	*vain ajid muhandisan*	وين أجد مهندسا
Where can I find a doctor?	*vain ajid tabeeban*	وين أجد طبيبا
Where can I find a note book?	*vain ajid daftaran*	وين أجد دفترا
Where can I find a room?	*vain ajid gurfah*	وين أجد غرفة
Where can I find Mr. Hashim?	*vain ajid assayyid Hashim*	وين أجد السيد هاشم
Where can I find a teacher?	*vain ajid mudarrisan*	وين أجد مدرسا
Where can I find an accountant?	*vain ajid muhasiban*	وين أجد محاسبا
Where can I find a nurse?	*vain ajid mumarridan*	وين أجد ممرضا
Where can I find a bus?	*vain ajid bassan*	وين أجد باصا
Where can I find a car?	*vain ajid sayyarah*	وين أجد سيارة
Where can I find a cycle?	*vain ajid darrajah*	وين أجد دراجة

How	*kayfa*	كيف
How are you?	*kayfa halaka*	كيف حالك
How are you?	*kayfaka*	كيفك
How do you go home?	*kayfa tarooh bayt*	كيف ترح بيت

81

How do you go to the office?	*kayfa tarooh maktab*	كيف ترح مكتب
How do you go hospital?	*kayfa tarooh mustashfa*	كيف ترح مستشفى
How do you come?	*kayfa tajee*	كيف تجيئ
How do you make arrangement?	*kayfa savvi tarteeb*	كيف سو ترتيب
How to close this	*kayfa sakkar hada*	كيف سكر هذا
How to open this	*kayfa batal hada*	كيف بطل هذا
How is your father	*kayfa babaa*	كيف بابا
How is your mother?	*kayfa maamaa*	كيف ماما
How is your wife?	*kayfazzoujat*	كيف الزوجة
How is your husband?	*keyfa zzouj*	كيف الزوج
How are your children?	*kayfal aulad*	كيف الأولاد
How is your job?	*kayfashugal*	كيف الشغل
How is the weather?	*kayfa taqas*	كيف الطقس
How is the business?	*kayfatijarah*	كيف التجارة
How is everything?	*kayfal umoor*	كيف الأمور
Who	*meen*	من / مين
Who are you?	*min inta*	مين إنت
Who is he?	*min huwa*	مين هو
Who is she?	*min hiya*	مين هي

Who is your calssmate?	*min zameeluka*	مين زميلك
Who is your friend?	*min sadeequka*	مين صديقك
Who is your partner?	*min shareekuka*	مين شريكك
Who is your father	*min abooka*	مين أبوك
Who is your brother?	*min akhooka*	مين أخوك
Who is your teacher?	*min mudarrisuka*	مين مدرسك
Who is your doctor?	*min tabeebuka*	مين طبيبك
Who is the manager of the company	*min mudeerushsharika*	مين مدير الشركة
Who is your guide	*min murshiduka*	مين مرشدك
Who is your supervisor?	*min mushrifuka*	مين مشرفك
Who is your Manager/principal	*min mudeeruka*	مين مديرك
Who is your neighbour?	*min jaruka*	مين جارك
Who is your leader?	*min imamuk*	مين إمامك
Who is your Engineer?	*min muhandisuka*	مين مهندسك
Who is your accountant?	*min muhasibuka*	مين محاسبك
Who is your sponsor?	*min kafeeluka*	مين كفيلك
Who is your nominee?	*min murashihuka*	مين مرشحك
Who is your follower?	*min tabi'uka*	مين تابعك
Who is your assistant?	*min musa'iduka*	مين مساعدك
Who is your observer?	*min muraqibuka*	مين مراقبك
Who made a call?	*minsavvi telephone*	مين سوي تلفون

Who wrote here?	min kataba hinee	مين كتب هني
Who sat there?	min jalasa hinaka	مين جلس هناك
Who spoiled this?	min fasada hada	مين فسد هذا
Who made a quarrel?	min savvi jinjaal	مين سوي جنجال
Who closed the door	min sakkaral baab	مين سكر الباب
Who opened the window?	min batalashubbak	مين بطل الشباك
Who registered first?	min sajjal avval	مين سجل أول
Who booked yesterday?	min hajaza ams	مين حجز أمس
Who came in the morning?	min yajee subhan	مين يجيء صبحا
Who spoke over telephone?	min kallam bitalaphoon	مين كلم بالتلفون
Who taught you Quran?	min 'allamakal quran	مين علمك القرآن
Who taught you Arabic?	min allamakal arabiyya	مين علمك العربية
Who taught you English?	min 'allamakal injleeziyya	مين علمك الإنجليزية
Who taught you Medicine?	min 'allamakatibb	مين علمك الطب
Who taught you Engineering?	min 'allamakal handasah	مين علمك الهندسة
Who taught you history	min 'allamaktaareekh	مين علمك التاريخ
Who taught you geography?	min 'allamakal jugrafiyah	مين علمك الجغرافية

Who assisted you in this?	*min sa'adaka fee hada*	مين ساعدك في هذا
Who cheated you?	*min khanaka*	مين خانك
Who signed?	*min vaqq'a*	مين وقع
Who troubled you?	*min dayyaqaka*	مين ضيقك

Whose / who   *meen*   مين

If *meen* is used in the middle of a sentence we will get the meaning whose. For whom also we can use this interrogative.

See the examples:

Whose car is this?	*sayyarah meen hadihi*	سيارة مين هذه
Whose house is this?	*baythi meen hada.*	بيت من هذا
Whose bag is this?	*haqeeba meen hadihi*	حقيبة مين هذه
Whose room is that?	*gurfatu meen tilka*	غرفة من تلك
Whose son is he?	*ibnu meen huwa*	إبن مين هو
Whose daughter is she?	*bintu meen hiya*	بنت مين هي
Whose shop is that?	*mahallu meen dalika*	محل مين ذلك
Whose hotel is this?	*funduqu meen hada*	فندق مين هذا
Whose office is this?	*makthabu meen hada*	مكتب مين هذا
Whose note book is this?	*daftaru meen hada*	دفتر مين هذا
Whose pen is this?	*qalamu meen hada*	قلم مين هذا
Whose book is this?	*kitab meen hada*	كتاب مين هذا
Whose suitcase is this?	*shantatu meen hadihi*	شنطة مين هذه
Who with you go?	*ma'a meen tarooh*	مع مين ترح

Who with you play?	ma'a meen tal'ab	مع مين تلعب
Who with you sleep?	ma'a meen tanaam	مع مين تنام
Who with you sit?	ma'a meen tajlis	مع مين تجلس
Who with you work?	m'a meen tashtagil	مع مين تشتغل
Who with you dance?	ma'a meen tarqus	مع مين ترقص
Who with you talk?	ma'a meen tatakallam	مع مين تتكلم
Who with you study?	ma'a meen tadrusu	مع مين تدرس
who with you discuss?	ma'a meen tanaqash	مع مين تناقش
Who with you compete?	ma'a meen tunafisu	مع مين تنافس
Who do you want?	tabgee meen	تبغ مين
Whom did you speak with?	ma'a meen kallamt	مع مين كلمت
Whom did you help?	saa'adta meen	ساعدت مين
Whom did you sponsor?	kafalta meen	كفلت مين
Whom did you see?	shufta meen	شفت مين

Howmany / howmuch	**kam**	كم
Howmany books have you got?	kam kitaban 'indaka	كم كتابا عندك؟
Howmany pens have you got?	kam qalaman 'indaka	كم قلما عندك؟
howmany children have you got?	kam valadan 'indaka	كم ولدا عندك؟
Howmany cars have you got?	kam sayyara 'indaka	كم سيارة عندك؟

86

Howmany cows have you got?	*kam baqarah 'indaka*	كم بقرة عندك؟
Howmany (howmuch) you want?	*kam tabgi*	كم تبغ
Howmuch is the discount	*khasm kam*	خصم كم
How old are you?	*kam umruka*	كم عمرك
Howmany rooms are there?	*kam gurfa fee*	كم غرفة فيه
Howmany toilets are there?	*kam hammam fee*	كم حماما فيه
Howmany days you want?	*kam yauman tabgee*	كم يوما تبغ
What is the last price?	*aakhir kam*	آخر كم
What time do you come?	*saa'a kam tajee*	ساعة كم تجيء؟
What time do you go?	*saa'a kam tarooh*	ساعة كم ترح؟
What time is the flight	*saa'a kam ataa'irah*	ساعة كم الطائرة؟
What time is the train?	*saa'a kam alqitaar*	ساعة كم القطار؟
What time does it close?	*saa'a kam sakkar*	ساعة كم سكر؟
What time did you make telephone?	*saa'a kam savvee telephone*	ساعة كم سوي تلفون؟
Howmany persons have registered?	*kam nafar sajjala*	كم نفر سجل؟
Howmuch have you got?	*kam ma'aka*	كم معك؟
Howmuch I owe you?	*kam laka*	كم لك؟

| For how much did you buy this cow? | *bikam ishtaraita hadihil baqarah* | بكم إشتريت هذه البقرة؟ |
| For how much is that chair? | *bikam dalikal kursee* | بكم ذلك الكرسي |

When	*mataa*	متى
When does the manager come?	*mataa yajee'ul mudeer*	متى يجيء المدير؟
When does the manager go?	*mataa yaruh al mudeer*	متى يرح المدير؟
When did you call?	*mataa savvi theliphoon*	متى سو تلفون؟
When does the gate close?	*mata sakkaral baab*	متى سكر الباب؟
When does the library open?	*mata batalal maktaba*	متى بطل المكتبة؟
When is your vacation?	*mata ijazatuka*	متى إجازتك؟
When is your wedding party?	*mata valeematuka*	متى وليمتك؟
When is your duty?	*mata davamuka*	متى دوامك؟
When is your examination?	*mata imtihanuka*	متى إمتحانك؟
When are you going to your country?	*mata taruh bilad*	متى ترح بلاد؟
When will you come from your country?	*mata tajee minal bilad*	متى تجيء من البلاد؟
When do you call your wife?	*mata tatasil bi zoujatika*	متى تتصل بزوجتك؟

When will you pay the fee?	*mata tadfaurrusoom*	متى تدفع الرسوم؟
When will you pay the penalty?	*mata tadfa'ul garama*	متى تدفع الغرامة؟
When do you watch TV?	*mata tushahidutalfaz*	متى تشاهد التلفاز؟
When do you play?	*mata tal'ab*	متى تلعب؟
When do you visit your relatives?	*mata tazooru aqaribak*	متى تزور أقاربك؟
When will you buy a car?	*mata tashtaree sayyarah*	متى تشتري سيارة؟
When will you come to my house?	*mata tajee ilaa baytee*	متى تجيئ إلى بيتي؟
When will you invite me to your house?	*ata tad'oonee ilaa baytika*	متى تدعوني الى بيتك؟
When will the examination result appear?	*ata tadharu nateejatul imtihan*	متى تظهر نتيجة الامتحان؟
When do you write your home work?	*mataa taktubul vajibat*	متى تكتب الواجبات؟
When do you memorise Quran?	*mataa tahfadul Qur'an*	متى تحفظ القرآن؟

Which	*ayye*	أي
Which pen you want?	*ayyu qalamin tabgi*	أي قلم تبغ؟
Which book do you read?	*ayyu kitabin taqrae*	أي كتاب تقرأ؟
In which school do you study?	*fee ayyi madrasa tadrusu*	في أي مدرسة تدرس؟

In which school do you work?	fee ayyi madrasa tashtagil	في أي مدرسة تشتغل؟
Which room do you want?	ayyu gurfa tabgee	أي غرفة تبغ؟
Which doctor do you go to?	ilaa ayyi daktoor taruh	الى أي دكتور ترح؟
Which office is the nearest?	ayyu maktabin aqrab	أي مكتب أقرب؟
Which hospital is the nearest?	ayyu mustashfa aqrab	أي مستشفى أقرب؟
Which shop do you like?	ayyu dukanin tuhibbı	أي دكان تحب؟
Which car do you buy?	ayyu sayyarah tashtaree	أي سيارة تشتري؟
Which city you live in?	fee ayyi madeena taskun	في أي مدينة تسكن؟
In which office do you work?	fee ayyi maktabin tashtagil	تشتغل؟ في أي مكتب
Which magazine do you read?	ayyu majalla taqra'	أي مجلة تقرأ؟
Take whichever you like	khud ayy shai' tabgee	خذ أي شيىء تبغ؟
Which one is better?	ayyuhumaa ahsan	أيهما أحسن؟
Which country you live in?	fee ayyi baladin taskunu	في أي بلد تسكن؟
Which country you travel to?	ilaa ayyi baladin tusafiru	إلى أي بلد تسافر؟
Which country are you returning from?	min ayyi baladin tarjee	من أي بلد ترجع؟

90

Which village do you live in?	fee ayyi qaryah taskunu	في أي قرية تسكن؟
Which dress do you like?	ayyu libasin tuhibbu	أي لباس تحب؟
Which story do you read?	ayyu qissa taqra'	أي قصة تقرأ؟

Why — *limada/leysh* — لماذا/ ليش

For 'why' the proper word is limada, but in spoken Arabic leysh is commonly used.

Why are you late?	leysh inta muta'akhir	ليش إنت متأخر؟
Why is he early?	leysh huwa mubakkir	ليش هو مبكر؟
Why does he come late?	leysh yajee muta'akhir	ليش يجيء متأخر؟
Why are you angry?	leysh inta za'lan	ليش إنت زعلان؟
Why are you angry?	leysh inta gadban	ليش إنت غضبان؟
Why didn't you attend the meeting?	leysh lam tahduril haflah	ليش لم تحضر الحفلة؟
Why didn't you contact?	lesh lam tatasil	ليش لم تتصل؟
Why did you close the door early?	leysh sakkaral baba mubakkir	ليش سكر الباب مبكر؟
Why didn't he come yesterday?	leysh ma yajee ams	ليش ما يجيء أمس؟
Why do you need money now?	leysh tabgee fuloos al'aan	ليش تبغ فلوس الآن؟
Why did not you make arrangement?	leysh ma savvee tarteeb	ليش ما سوى ترتيب؟
Why is he absent today?	leysh huwa ga'ibilyaum	ليش هو غائب اليوم؟

91

Why are you busy today?	*leysh inta mashgool alyaum*	ليش إنت مشغول اليوم؟
Why are you free?	*leysh inta fadee*	ليش إنت فاضى؟
Why do you go to the market?	*leysh taruh sooq*	ليش ترح سوق؟
Why didn't you pay the fee yet?	*leysh lam tadfa'irrusooma hatal aan*	ليش لم تدفع الرسوم حتى الآن؟
Why didn't you pay the fine yet?	*leysh lam tadfa'il garaama hattal aan*	ليش لم تدفع الغرامة حتى الآن؟
Why didn't you do the home work?	*leysh lam taktubil vajib*	ليش لم تكتب الواجب؟
Why didn't you read the lesson?	*leysh lam taqra'iddars*	ليش لم تقرإ الدرس؟
Why didn't you help the poor?	*leysh lam tusaa'idil faqeer*	ليش لم تساعد الفقير؟
Why didn't you play yesterday?	*leysh lam tal'ab ams*	ليش لم تلعب أمس؟
Why didn't you go home yesterday?	*leysh lam taruh albayta ams*	ليش لم ترح البيت أمس؟
Why didn't you inform father?	*leysh lam tukhbir babaa*	ليش لم تخبر بابا؟
Why do you write standing?	*leysh taktub qa'iman*	ليش تكتب قائما؟
Are / Is	***hal***	هل
Are you a student?	*hal inta taalib*	هل إنت طالب؟
yes, I am a student	*na'am, ana taalib*	نعم أنا طالب

92

No, I am a teacher	*la, ana mudarris*	لا أنا مدرس
are you married?	*hal inta mutazavvij*	هل إنت متزوج؟
yes, I am married	*na'am ana mutazavvij*	نعم أنا متزوج
No, I am bachelor	*la, ana a'zab*	لا أنا أعزب
Is he busy?	*hal huwa mashgool*	هل هو مشغول؟
Yes, he is busy	*na'am, huwa mashqool*	نعم هو مشغول
No, he is not busy	*la, huwa mush mashgool*	لا هو مش مشغول
No, he is free	*la huwa fadee*	لا هو فاضي
Are you staying alone?	*hal taskunu vahdaka*	هل تسكن وحدك؟
No, I stay with my family	*la, askunu maá aaílatee*	لا، أسكن مع عائلتي
Yes, I stay alone	*naám, askunu vahdee*	نعم أسكن وحدي
Is this your house?	*hal hadaa baytuka*	هل هذا بيتك؟
Yes, this is my house	*naám hada baytee*	نعم هذا بيتي
No, this is my brother's house	*la, hada baytu akhee*	لا هذا بيت أخي
Do you know Arabic?	*hal ta'rifu arabee*	هل تعرف عربي؟
Yes, I know	*naám araf*	نعم عرف
No, I don't know	*la ana maa áraf*	لا أنا ما عرف
I know little	*áraf shuai shuai*	عرف شوي شوي
Do you speak Arabic?	*hal tatakallam arabee*	هل تتكلم عربي؟

Do you understand Arabic?	*hal tafham arabee*	هل تفهم عربي؟
Do you know typing?	*hal ta'rifu tibaá*	هل تعرف الطباعة؟
Does anyone speak Arabic?	*hal yoojad ahad yatakallamu arabee*	هل يوجد أحد يتكلم عربي؟
Have you got a brother?	*hal laka akhun*	هل لك أخ؟
Have you got money?	*hal índaka fuloos*	هل عندك فلوس؟

Is	**'a**	**أ**
Is this his Office?	*a hada maktabuhu*	أهذا مكتبه؟
Yes, this is his office	*naám, hada maktabuh*	نعم هذا مكتبه
No, his office is that	*la, maktabuhu daka*	لا مكتبه ذاك
Did you do this?	*hal anta faálta hada*	أأنت فعلت هذا
Yes, I did this	*ayva, faáltu hada*	فعلت هذا أيوى
No, I did not do this	*la, ma faáltu hada*	لا ما فعلت هذا

LESSON SEVENTEEN

MAY BE / POSSIBLE / PLEASE etc.

Could you try?	*mumkin tuhavil*	ممكن تحاول؟
Could you try for me?	*mumkin tuhavil lee*	ممكن تحاول لي؟
May I help you?	*mumkin usaíduka*	ممكن أساعدك؟
Could you make the arrangement?	*mumkin savvi tarteeb*	ممكن سو ترتيب؟
Could I speak to the Manager?	*mumkin ukallimal mudeer*	ممكن أكلم المدير؟
Could I speak to him?	*mumkin ukallimahu*	ممكن أكلمه؟
Could you try for me once more?	*mumkin tuhavil lee marratani*	ممكن تحاول لي مرة ثاني؟
Could you give me time?	*mumkin tu'teeni vaqt*	ممكن تعطني وقت؟
Could you repeat the words?	*mumkin tukarriril kalam*	ممكن تكرر الكلام
Could I wait here?	*mumkin anthadiru hinee*	ممكن أنتظر هني؟
Could I sit there?	*mumkin ajlis hinaka*	ممكن أجلس هناك؟
Could you give me 1000 Riyal?	*mumkin tu'teeni alf riyal*	ممكن تعطني ألف ريال؟

Could you help me in this?	mumkin tusaídanee fee hada	ممكن تساعدني في هذا؟
Could you close the door?	mumkin sakkiril baab	ممكن سكر الباب؟
Could you make a copy of this?	mumkin savvi nuskha min haada	ممكن سو نسخة من هذا؟
Could we play football today?	mumkin naláb kurah alyaum	مكن نلعب كرة اليوم؟
Could you come with me to the Passport Office?	mumkin ta'tee maée ilal javvazat	ممكن تأتي معي الى الجوزات؟
Could we eat from the restaurant today?	mumkin na'kulal yauma minal matám	ممكن نأكل اليوم من المطعم؟
He might come late today	mumkin yajee alyaum mutaákhir	ممكن يجيء اليوم متأخرا
He may/might not come today	mumkin la yajee alyaum	ممكن لا يجيء اليوم
He might sign your papers today	mumkin vaqaá auraqaka alyaum	ممكن وقع أوراقك اليوم
He might go after some time	mumkin yaruh ba'da shuai	ممكن يرح بعد شوي
He may contact you later on	mumkin yatasil bika ba'dain	ممكن يتصل بك بعدين؟
It may finish today?	mumkin khallasil yaum	ممكن خلص اليوم
He may come day after tomorrow	mumkin yajee ba'da bukrah	ممكن يجيء بعد بكرة
It may rain today	mumkin yamtir alyaum	ممكن يمطر اليوم

96

Please	*min fadlik*	من فضلك
Close the door please	*min fadlika sakkiril baab*	من فضلك سكر الباب
Open the window please	*battal shubbaka min fadlika*	بطل الشباك من فضلك
Please help him in studies	*min fadlika saídhu fiddirasa*	من فضلك ساعده في الدراسة
Check the invoice please	*fatishil faatoorah min fadlika*	فتش الفاتورة من فضلك
Pay the fee please	*idfaírrusooma min fadlika*	إدفع الرسوم من فضلك
Please submit the application	*qaddimi talaba min fadlika*	قدم الطلب من فضلك
Please give me 100 Riyal	*min fadlika a'tinee miáth riyal*	من فضلك أعطني مائة ريال
Please bring tomorrow	*min fadlika jib bukrah*	من فضلك جب بكرة
Please go with him	*min fadlika ruh maáhu*	من فضلك رح معه
Please relax for a while	*min fadlika istarih shuvayy*	من فضلك إسترح شوي
Please	*arjooka*	أرجوك
Rama please	*arjooka yaa raamaa*	أرجوك يا راما
Please come to me tomorrow	*arjooka an ta'teeni bukrah*	أرجوك أن تأتيني بكرة
Please give me time	*arjooka an tu'teenee vaqt*	أرجوك أن تعطني وقت
Please don't disturb me	*arjooka an laa tuza'jinee*	أرجوك أن لا تزعجني

97

Please help me in this	arjooka an tusaidnee fee hada	أرجوك أن تساعدني في هذا
Please pay the fee first	yurjaa dafúrrusoom avvalan	يرجى دفع الرسوم أولا
Please pay the fine first	arrajau dafúl garama avvalan	الرجاء دفع الغرامة أولا
Please attend the meeting	yurjaa hudoorul haflah	يرجى حضور الحفلة
Please go out from here	yurjaa al khurooj min hinee	يرجى الخروج من هني
Please approve	arjoo muvafaqa	أرجو موافقة
Please forgive	arjoo samaaha	أرجو سماحة
Please make arrangements	arjooka savvi tarteebaat	أرجو سو ترتيبات

I am looking for	**abhathu 'an**	أبحث عن
I am looking for a teacher	abhathu án mudarris	بحث عن مدرس
I am looking for an accountant	abhathu án muhasib	بحث عن محاسب
I am looking for an engineer	abhathu án muhandis	بحث عن مهندس
I am looking for a girl friend	abhathu án sadeeqa	بحث عن صديقة
I am looking for a partner	abhathu án shareek	بحث عن شريك
I am looking for a project	abhathu an khutah	بحث عن خطة
I am looking for a house	abhathu án bayt	بحث عن بيت

If you don't mind   *lou samaht*   لو سمحت

If you don't mind, close the door	*lou samaht sakkiril baab*	لو سمحت سكر الباب
If you don't mind, give me time	*lou samaht a'tinee vaqt*	لو سمحت أعطني وقت
If you don't mind, find for him a maid	*lou samaht aoujid lahu khadimah*	لو سمحت أوجد له خادمة
If you don't mind, speed up the procedures	*lou samaht asriil ijraáat*	لو سمحت أسرع الاجرائات
If you don't mind, come tomorrow	*lou samaht taáal bukrah*	لو سمحت تعال بكرة
If you don't mind, drop me at the school	*lou samaht khallinee al madrasah*	لو سمحت خلني المدرسة
If you don't mind, drop him at the air port	*lou samaht vaddiúhul mataar*	لو سمحت ودعه المطار
If you don't mind, bring tea	*lou samaht jib shay*	لو سمحت جب شاي
If you don't mind, don't tell this to any one	*lou samaht la taqul hada li ahad*	لو سمحت لا تقل هذا لأحد
If you don't mind, take this from here	*lou samaht khud hada min hinee*	لو سمحت خذ هذا من هني
If you don't mind, pay the fee	*lou samaht idfairrusoom*	لو سمحت إدفع الرسوم
If you don't mind, help him in this	*lou samaht saidhu fee haadaa*	لو سمحت ساعده في هذا

If you don't mind, co-operate with him in this project	*lou samahth taáavun maáhu fee hadal mashrooe*	لو سمحت تعاون معه في هذا المشروع
If you don't mind, give me 1000 dollar	*lou samaht a'tinee alfa doolar*	لو سمحت اعطني ألف دولار
If you don't mind, come with me to the office	*lou samaht taáal maée ilal maktab*	لو سمحت تعال معي الى المكتب
If you don't mind, consult him	*lou samaht shavir maáhu*	لو سمحت شاور معه
If you don't mind, make arrangements today	*lou samaht savvi tarteeb alyaum*	لو سمحت سو ترتيب اليوم
If you don't mind, make it fast	*lou samaht savvi surá*	لو سمحت سو سرعة
If you don't mind, correct the papers now	*lou samaht sahhihil auraq aláan*	لو سمحت صحح الأوراق الآن
If you don't mind, contact him now	*lou samaht itasal bihee alheen*	لو سمحت إتصل به الحين
If you don't mind, reserve a ticket for me	*lou samaht ahjiz lee tadkirah*	لو سمحت أحجز لي تذكرة
If you don't mind, give me special discount	*lou samaht a'tinee khasm khas*	لو سمحت أعطني خصم خاص
If you don't mind, give him this	*lou samaht a'etihi hada*	لو سمحت أعطه هذا

LESSON EIGHTEEN

CONVERSATIONAL PRACTICE

Now let us try to come to the actual conversation. I'm giving ten model conversations as guide lines for the beginners. Most of these are based on written patterns, but there are good numbers of words and phrases that can be used in spoken language as well.

1. In the school   *fil madrasa*   في المدرسة

Ahmed: Good Morning, Khalid	أحمد: صباح الخير يا خالد
Khalid: Good Morning, How are you?	خالد: صباح النور، كيف حالك؟
Ahmed: Fine, praise be to Allah, and what about you?	أحمد: بخير ألحمد لله، وأنت كيف حالك؟
Khalid: Fine, praise be to Allah, How is your Family? How is your father? How is your mother and children?	خالد:طيب والحمد لله، وكيف عائلتك، كيف بابا، كف ماما وكيف الأولاد؟
Ahmed: All are fine, praise be to Allah, what do you do here Khalid?	أحمد : كلهم طيبون والحمد لله, شو سوي هني يا خالد؟
Khalid: My son is studying in this school. I came to enquire about his studies, and what do you do here?	خالد : إبني دارس في هذه المدرسة، جئت لأبحث عن دراسته وأنت شو سوي هني؟

Ahmed: My son is also studying in this school. I came to drop him. Since when your son is in this school?

أحمد: إبني أيضا دارس في هذه المدرسة جئت كي أودعه ، من متى إبنك في هذه المدرسة؟

Khalid: He joined in this school since the beginning of the current academic year. When did you admit your son?

خالد : التحق بهذه المدرسة من بداية العام الدراسي الجاري ، ومتى ادخلت إبنك؟

Ahmed: I admitted him day before yesterday, in which class your son is studying?

أحمد: أدخلته أول أمس ، في أي صف يدرس إبنك؟

Khalid: He is in fifth Standard. In which class your son is studying?

خالد : هو في الصف الخامس الابتدائي وفي أي صف يدرس إبنك؟

Ahmed: He is in IVth Standard. What is the name of your son?

أحمد: هو في الصف الرابع الابتدائي، شسم إبنك؟

Khalid: His name is Abdullah, and your son, what is his name?

خالد : إسمه عبد الله، وإبنك شسمه؟

Ahmed: His name is Abdurahman. What is the name of Abdulla's teacher?

أحمد: إسمه عبد الرحمن، شسم مدرس عبد الله؟

Khalid: His teacher is Dr. Easa. What is the name of the teacher of Abdurahman?

خالد : مدرسه د.عيسى وعبد الرحمن شسم مدرسه؟

Ahmed: A lady teacher is teaching him. Her name is Rasheeda Abul Jalal. Do you know the house of the teacher?

أحمد: تدرسه مدرسة. إسمها رشيدة أبو الجلال. هل تدري بيت المدرس؟

102

Khalid: I don't know. They say his house is near the school. Do you know the house of the principal?

خالد : أنا ما عرف. يقولون بيته قريب من المدرسة. وأنت تعرف بيت المدير؟

Ahmed: Yes, his house is near my house. Do you need any assistance?

أحمد: أيوا ، بيته قريب من بيتي. هل تريد أي مساعدة

Khalid: No, thanks, where are you going from here?

خالد : لا، شكرا. وين ترح من هنى؟

Ahmed: I wan to go to the market. Do you want to accompany me to the market?

أحمد: أبغ أرح إلى السوق تبغي ترافقني إلى السوق؟

Khalid: To which market do you go?

خالد : أي سوق ترح؟

Ahmed: I am going to the vegetable market.

أحمد: أرح سوق الخضر.

Khalid: How do you go to the market?

خالد : كيف ترح السوق؟

Ahmed: I have got a car. Have you got a car?

أحمد: عندي سيارة. هل عندك سيارة؟

Khalid: No, I don't hve a car. My house is near to the school. I will go walking

خالد : لا ما عندي سيارة. بيتي قريب من المدرسة. أرح ماشيا.

Ahmed: When will you go to the factory?

أحمد : متى ترح إلى المصنع؟

Khalid: I will go at 9.00 AM, and when will you go to the company?	خالد : أرح الساعة التاسعة صباحا. وأنت متى ترح إلى الشركة؟
Ahmed: I will go at 8.30 AM, How do you go to the factory?	أحمد: أروح الساعة الثامنة و النصف صباحا. كيف ترح إلى المصنع؟
Khalid: I will go in the factory's bus, and how do you go to the company?	خالد : أروح في باص المصنع وأنت كيف تروح إلى الشركة؟
Ahmed: I will go in my car.	أحمد: أروح في سيارتي.
Khalid: Have you got a driver also?	خالد : عندك سائق أيضا؟
Ahmed: No, my car is not big. I drive it myself. What time do you return from the factory?	أحمد: لا ، سيارتي مب كبيرة. أسوقها بنفسي. ساعة كم ترجع من المصنع؟
Khalid: Usually I return from the factory at 4.00 PM. Sometimes I work overtime. What time do you return from the company?	خالد : أرجع من المصنع عادة الساعة الرابعة مساء، وأحيانا أعمل ساعات إضافية. ساعة كم ترجع من الشركة يا أحمد؟
Ahmed: Sometimes I return at 1.00 PM and sometimes at 2.00 PM.	أحمد : أحيانا أرجع الساعة الواحدة بعد الزوال، وأحيانا الساعة الثانية.
Khalid: Do you go to the factory again?	خالد : هل تذهب إلى الشركة مرة أخرى؟

Ahmed: No, I will not go again. My son will supervise the company in the afternoon. Where are you Khalid? I didn't see you for a long time. How many children have you got now?

أحمد : لا، انا لا أذهب إليها مرة أخرى يشرف عليها إبني بعد الظهر. وينك يا خالد من زمان أنا ما شفتك. كم ولد عندك الحين؟

Khalid: I am very busy in the factory. I will go home after the duty, and I will supervise the studies of my children. I have three sons and three daughters. Zubair is the eldest and is studying for engineering at the Government college. Abdul Hakeem is studying in the secondary school and Abdullah is studying in the primary school. All daughters are teachers in the middle school, and how many children have you got, Ahmed?

خالد : أنا مشغول واجد في المصنع أروح البيت بعد الدوام وأشرف على دراسة الأولاد. عندي ثلاثة أولاد وثلاث بنات. زبير هو أكبر منهم. ويدرس الهندسة في الكلية الحكومة وعبد الحكيم يدرس في المدرسة الثانوية وعبد الله يدرس في المدرسة الابتدائية. وأما البنات وكلهم مدرسات في المدرسة المتوسطة. وأنت كم ولدا عندك يا أحمد؟

Ahmed: I have two children. Abdurahman and Abdurazak. Both of them are studying in the Praimary School. I am going. I have a meeting in the company today. I will see you after words, Khalid. Good bye.

أحمد : عندي ولدان. عبد الرحمن و عبد الرزاق وهما يدرسان في المدرسة الابتدائية. أروح عندي إجتماع في الشركة اليوم. أشوفك بعدين يا خالد. مع السلامة.

Khalid: Good bye, See you.

خالد : مع السلامة، إلى اللقاء.

2. In the hospital   *fil mustashfa*   في المستشفى

Babu: Good Evening	بابو : مساء الخير
Reception: Good Evening, how are you? Can I help you?	مؤظف الاستقبال : مساء النور، كيف حالك؟ ممكن اساعدك؟
Babu: Fine, Praise be to Allah, I want to see the Cardiologist	بابو : زين الحمد لله، أبغ أشف دكتور القلب.
Reception: Have you got a health card?	مؤظف الاستقبال : عندك بطاقة الصحة؟
Babu: No, I am new in the country. I don't have a health card. How can I get the health card?	بابو : لا، أنا جديد في البلاد. ليس عندي بطاقة الصحة؟
Reception: Have you got residence permit?	مؤظف الاستقبال : هل عندك رخصة الاقامة؟
Babu: Yes, it is there.	بابو : أيوا موجود.
Reception: OK, there is no problem. Take this form, fill in the details and submit it in that counter Then pay 100 Riyal. They will give you a receipt and that is enough for treatment.	مؤظف الاستقبال : زين ما في مشكلة، خذ هذه الاستمارة. أكمل البيانات وقدم في الشباك هناك، بعدين إدفع مائة ريال، وهم يعطونك إيصال. وهذا يكفي للعلاج
Babu: Thanks, I will complete the formalities now and come.	بابو : شكرا، أكمل الاجراءات الحين، وأتي.

Reception: Hello, welcome.	مؤظف الاستقبال : أهلا و سهلا
Babu: Here is my receipt	بابو : هذا إيصالي.
Reception: OK, What is your name? How old are you?	مؤظف الاستقبال : زين، شسمك؟ كم عمرك؟
Babu: Babu – 52	بابو : باب ٢ ٥
Reception: Your number is 22. Please sit there.	مؤظف الاستقبال : رقمك ٢٢ إسترح هناك.
Babu: Thank you so much.	بابو : شكرا جزيلا
Reception: You are welcome	مؤظف الاستقبال : عفوا
Babu: Good evening doctor.	بابو : مساء الخير يا دكتور.
Doctor: Good evening, how are you?	دكتور : مساء النور. كيف حالك؟
Babu: Good, doctor! I am new to the country. I have too much pain in the heart	بابو : بخير دكتور ، أنا جديد في البلاد . لي ألم واجد في القلب
Doctor: Are you a smoker?	دكتور : هل أنت مدخن؟
Babu: Sometimes.	بابو : أحيانا.
Doctor: No way, you should quit	دكتور : لا يسير ، لازم تقلع.
Babu: I will try, Insha Allah	بابو : أحاول ان شاء الله
Doctor: When did the pain start?	دكتور : متى بدأ الألم؟
Babu: Day before yesterday	بابو : أول أمس

Doctor: Why you didn't come first. What did you do? Did yo take any medicine?

دكتور : ليش لم تجئ أول، شسويت هل أخذت أي دواء؟

Babu: I did not do anything.

بابو : أنا ما سويت شيئا

Doctor: Sit here, let me see.

دكتور : إجلس هني، خلني شف.

Doctor: No problem Babu, This is due to gas. Take this medicine.

دكتور : ما في مشكلة يا بابو، هذا من الغاز. خذ هذا الدواء

Babu: How many times?

بابو : كم مرة؟

Doctor: Three times a day.

دكتور : ثلاث مرات في اليوم

Babu: Before food or after food?

بابو : قبل الأكل أو بعده؟

Doctor: Take before food

دكتور : خذ قبل الأكل.

Babu: From where I will get the medicine?

بابو : من أين حصل الدواء؟

Doctor: Take it from the Pharmacy. Have you got any other problem Babu?

دكتور : خذ من الصيدلية. لك أي مشكلة أخرى يا بابو؟

Babu: No other problem. Praise be to Allah.

بابو : ما في شيء أخر. الحمد لله.

Doctor: Don't worry. This is simple. May Allah cure you

دكتور : لا تخف، هذا بسيط، شفاك الله.

Babu: Thank you doctor.

بابو : شكرا يا دكتور.

Doctor: Welcome

دكتور : عفوا.

Babu: How many days should I take this medicine?	بابو : كم يوما أخذ هذا الدواء؟
Doctor: Take it three days and I want to see you after words	خذ هذا ثلاثة أيام. وأبغي أشفك بعد.
Babu: OK	بابو : زين.
Doctor: Good bye	دكتور : في أمان الله.
Babu: Good bye	بابو : مع السلامة.

3. At a travel agent's office	*fee maktabi ssafariyath*	في مكتب السفريات
Babu : Good morning		بابو : صباح الخير
Agent : Good morning, How are you?		مؤظف السفريات : صباح النور، كيف حالك؟
Babu : Good, praise to be Allah		بابو: بخير ، الحمد لله
Agent : Please come and take your seat.		مؤظف السفريات : فضل إسترح.
Agent : Can I help you		مؤظف السفريات : ممكن أساعدك؟
Babu : I want to travel to India		بابو: أبغ أسافر الهند.
Agent : When do you want to travel?		مؤظف السفريات: متى تبغ أن تسافر؟
Babu : By the end of June.		بابو : في نهاية يونو.
Agent : To which Airport you would like to travel?		مؤظف السفريات: أي مطار تبغ تسافر؟

Babu: I would like to travel to Calicut	بابو: أبغ أسافر إلى كالكوت.
Agent : Which flight you want?	مؤظف السفريات: أي طائرة تبغ؟
Babu: Is there any difference in charge?	بابو : في فرق في الأجور؟
Agent : Indirect flight there is a discount of 15 %	مؤظف السفريات: طائرة غير مواجهة في خسم %١٥
Babu: What are the available flights to Calicut?	بابو : شن الطائرات الموجودة إلى كالكوت؟
Agent : Indian Airlines, Qatar Airways, Kuwait Airways and Srilanka Airlines are available. Tell me the exact date of your journey.	مؤظف السفريات: الهندية، والقطرية، والكويتية، وسريلنكية، قل لي يوم السفر بالضبط.
Babu: I want to travel on 29th / 30th of June.	بابو : أبغ أسافر في ٢٩ أو ٣٠ يونو
Agent : Sorry Babu! Tickets in all flights during these days are booked long back. I will register your name in the waiting list and try to give you a seat.	مؤظف السفريات : أسف يا بابو، التذاكر في الطائرات كلها في هذه الأيام محجوزة من زمان. أسجل إسمك في قائمة الانتظار وأحاول أن أعطيك تذكرة.
Babu : Please try for me.	بابو : من فضلك حاول لي.
Agent : Are you travelling alone?	مؤظف السفريات : هل أنت مسافر وحدك؟

Babu : No, I am traveling along with my family.

بابو: أنا مسافر مع العائلة.

Agent : Howmany tickets you want

مؤظف السفريات: كم تذكرة تبغ؟

Babu : I want five tickets.

بابو : أبغ خمس تذاكر.

Agent : Five tickets are difficult in June end. Anyway I will try for you.

مؤظف السفريات : خمس تذاكر مشكلة في نهاية يونو، علي كل حال أحاول لك.

Babu : I have to travel by the end ‹ June after the school closes.

بابو : لازم أسافر في نهاية يونو، بعد ما سكر المدرسة.

Agent : Well, give me the details

مؤظف السفريات: زين، أعطيني البنايات.

Babu : Ask me what you want?

بابو : إسألني شن تبغ؟

Agent : Your name, address, telephone number and names of others who are traveling with you?

مؤظف السفريات : شسمك؟ عنوان؟ رقم التلفون؟ أسماء الأخرين الذين يسافرون معك.

Babu : Babu Varghese, PO Box. 2836, Tel: 4652624, My wife Leela and my children Jaison, George and Clint.

بابو : بابو ورغيس ص ب: ٢٨٣٦ هاتف: ٤٦٥٢٦٢٤ زوجتي ليلة، وابنائي جيسن وجورج وكلنت.

Agent : What are the ages of your children?

مؤظف السفريات : أولادك كم اعمارهم؟

Babu : Jaison 18, George 12 and Clint 8 years

بابو : جيسن ١٨ وجورج ١٢ وكلنت ٨ سنوات.

111

Agent : Are all children students?

مؤظف السفريات : الأولاد كلهم طلاب؟

Babu : Yes, they are students of Ideal Indian School.

بابو : أيوا هم طلاب المدرسة الهندية المثالية.

Agent : Fine, Bring a letter from the school and get the signature of the school principal on this form. You may get 25 % discount on their tickets.

مؤظف السفريات : زين، جب خطاب من المدرسة وتوقيع من مدير المدرسة في هذه الاستمارة عشان حصل ٢٥ %خصم في تذاكرهم.

Babu : I will bring it to you tomorrow or day after tomorrow

بابو : أجب لك بكرة أو بعد بكرة.

Agent : Tomorrow is better. Don't be late.

مؤظف السفريات : بكرة أحسن، لا تتأخر.

Babu : Fine, What time does your office open in the morning?

بابو : زين ، ساعة كم بطل مكتبكم في الصباح؟

Agent : At 8:30 AM

مؤظف السفريات : ٨:٣٠

Babu : What time does it close?

بابو : ساعة كم سكر ؟

Agent : At 1:00 PM

مؤظف السفريات : الساعة الواحدة بعد الزوال.

Babu : What time does your office open in the evening?

بابو : ساعة كم بطل مكتبكم في المساء؟

Agent : At 4:00 PM

مؤظف السفريات: ساعة أربعة.

Babu : What time does it close?

بابو : ساعة كم سكر؟

Agent : At 8:00 PM

مؤظف السفريات : الساعة الثامنة ليلا

Babu : I shall come in the evening.	بابو : أجيء في المساء.
Agent : As you like it	مؤظف السفريات : على كيفك؟
Babu : What time is the departure of Kuwait Airways from Doha?	بابو : مغادرة الكويتية ساعة كم من الدوحة؟
Agent : At 7:00 PM	مؤظف السفريات : ساعة ٧ مساء.
Babu : What time we reach Kuwait?	بابو : ساعة كم نصل الكويت؟
Agent : May be at 8:00 PM	مؤظف السفريات : ممكن الساعة الثامنة
Babu : Dinner from where?	بابو : العشاء مين وين؟
Agent : They may give you in Kuwait.	مؤظف السفريات : ممكن تعطون في الكويت.
Babu : How many hours waiting in Kuwait?	بابو : كم ساعة إنتظار في الكويت؟
Agent : Two hours	مؤظف السفريات : ساعتين.
Babu : What time is departure from there?	بابو : ساعة كم مغادرة من هناك؟
Agent : At 10:00 PM	مؤظف السفريات : الساعة العاشرة ليلا
Babu : OK, try for my tickets in Kuwait Airways.	بابو : زين ، حاول لي التذاكر في الكويتية.
Agent : Let me see	مؤظف السفريات : خلني شف
Babu : What time should I contact you?	بابو : متى أتصل بك؟

Agent : Check with me tomorrow morning	مؤظف السفريات : راجعني صباح بكرة
Babu : I will contact you in the morning	بابو : سأتصل بك صباحا؟
Agent : Good bye	مؤظف السفريات : مع السلامة.
Babu : See you	بابو : الى اللقاء.

4. At the bank   *fil bank*   في البنك

Fuvad : Good morning	فواد : صباح الخير
Bank Clerk : Good morning, Can I help you?	كاتب البنك : صباح النور. ممكن أساعدك؟
Fuvad : I want to open an account in your branch	فواد : أبغ أفتح حساب في فرعكم.
Bank Clerk : Where do you work?	كاتب البنك : أنت تشتغل وين؟
Fuvad : I am a teacher at the Ideal Indian School	فواد : أنا مدرس بالمدرسة الهندية المثالية.
Bank Clerk : How do you get the salary?	كاتب البنك : حصل المعاش كيف؟
Fuvad : From the accounts department of the school	فواد : من قسم حسابات المدرسة.
Bank Clerk : Will it be possible to transfer to the Bank?	كاتب البنك : ممكن تحولونه إلى البنك؟
Fuvad : I will submit an application to the principal; I think they will not object	فواد : أقدم الطلب إلى المدير، أعتقد وهم لا يمانعونه.

Bank Clerk : OK, go to the principal and speak to him. Let me know what he says?

كاتب البنك : زين، رح إلى المدير وكلمه وأخبرني ايش يقول.

Fuvad : I will come to you tomorrow

فواد : أني إليك بكرة.

Bank Clerk : As you like it.

كاتب البنك : على كيفك.

Fuvad : What are the papers required for opening the account?

فواد : ايش الأوراق اللازمة لفتح الحساب؟

Bank Clerk : A copy of Passport, a recent passport size photograph and a letter from the employer.

كاتب البنك : صورة من جواز السفر، صورة شخصية حديثة، وخطاب من طرف العمل.

Fuvad : OK

فواد : زين

Bank Clerk : Do you need any other service?

كاتب البنك : تبغ أي خدمة أخرى؟

Fuvad : I want a draft for Rs. 50,000/-

فواد : أبغ حوالة لخمسين ألف روبية.

Bank Clerk : Which bank you need?

كاتب البنك : أي بنك تبغ؟

Fuvad : Any bank, no problem, what is the exchange rate today?

فواد : أي بنك ما في مشكلة، شن سعر التحويلة اليوم؟

Bank Clerk : 80 Riyals for Rs. 1,000

كاتب البنك : ٨٠ ريال لألف روبية.

Fuvad : Where from I can get the draft?

فواد : مين وين حصل الحوالة؟

Bank Clerk : From the first

كاتب البنك : أول شباك في

115

counter on your right
اليمين.

Fuvad : Thanks
فؤاد : شكرا

Bank Clerk : Welcome.
كاتب البنك : عفوا

5. At the market   *fissooq*   في السوق

Ahmed : Assalamu Alaikkum
أحمد : السلام عليكم

Khalid : Wa Alaikkumussalam, How are you Ahmed?
خالد : وعليكم السلام، كيف حالك يا أحمد؟

Ahmed : Fine, praise be to Allah, and how are you?
أحمد : بخير والحمد لله، وأنت كيف حالك؟

Khalid : Fine, praise be to Allah what do you do here Ahmed?
خالد : زين، ألحمد لله. شو سوي هني يا أحمد؟

Ahmed : I am traveling after one week. I want to buy something to the children
أحمد : أنا مسافر بعد أسبوع، أبغ اشتري بعض الأغراض للأولاد.

Khalid : Well, go straight. See the first shop on your left. There is discount sale. There are valuable prizes also.
خالد : زين، رح سيتا، شف أول محل في اليسار، فيه تنزيلات وفيه جوائز قيمة بعد.

Ahmed : Is there special offer also.
أحمد : فيه عرض خاص بعد،

Khalid : I don't know, you see. What do you do here Ahmed?
خالد : أنا ما عرف، شف. وأنت شو سوي هني يا أحمد؟

Ahmed : I want to buy a gift to present to my friend on the occasion of his marriage
أحمد : أبغي اشتري هدية لصديقي لاقدمه في مناسبة زواجه.

Khalid : What type of gift you want?

خالد : أي هدية تبغ؟

Ahmed : Watch or anything else.

أحمد : ساعة أو أي شيئ آخر.

Khalid : Well, my neighbour has a shop in this market. He is an agen for watches. He may give you special discount on watches.

خالد : زين في هذا السوق محل لجاري هو وكيل الساعات، ممكن يعطيك خصم خاص في الساعات.

Ahmed : Could you introduce me to him.

أحمد : ممكن عرفني له.

Khalid : No Problem, Have you got a mobile?

خالد : ما ليش، عندك جوال؟

Ahmed : Ya, Here is it.

أحمد : أيوا موجود، ها هو ذا جوالي.

Khalid : I will speak to him now

خالد : أكلمه الحين.

Khalid : Assalamu alaikum Sajid, How are you? How are your children? Hope you are fine, How is your business?

خالد : السلام عليكم يا ساجد، شلونك، شخبارك، كيف الصحة؟ عساك طيب، وكيف الأولاد؟ كيف التجارة؟

Sajid : Fine, Praise be to Allah, Where are you Khalid? No visit, no telephone?

ساجد : بخير والحمد لله، وينك يا خالد، ما في زيارة ولا تلفون؟

Khalid : Very busy, no time.

خالد : مشغول واجد، ما في وقت.

Sajid : You need anything?

ساجد : تبغ شيئ؟

Khalid : Yes, I,m sending my friend Ahmed to you. He want a nice watch, give him special price.

خالد : اي، أرسل زميلي أحمد إليك يبغ ساعة زينة، أعطه سعر خاص.

Sajid : No problem, let him come now. I am there in the shop.

ساجد : ما في مشكلة إن شاء الله. خل يجي الحين أنا موجود في المحل.

Khalid : Well, I will send him now

خالد : زين، أرسله الحين.

Ahmed : How are you?

أحمد : السلام عليكم، كيف حالك؟

Sajid : Most welcome, please come, are you friend of Khalid He spoke to me now.

ساجد : وعليكم السلام، اهلا وسهلا. يا مرحباً تفضل، أنت صديق خالد؟ هو كلمني الحين.

Ahmed : Ya!

أحمد : أيوا

Sajid : Look which watch you want?

ساجد : شف أي ساعة تبغ؟

Ahmed : I want a nice watch. Is there Continental watch with you?

أحمد : أبغ ساعة زينة، فيه ساعة كونتيننتل عندكم؟

Sajid : Of course. Look there. All those are models of continental.

ساجد : طبعا، شف هناك. تلك كلها أنواع من كونتننتل.

Ahmed : Howmuch is this?

أحمد : هذه كم؟

Sajid : It is expensive, I will give you for 500/-

ساجد : هذه غالية، أعطيك بخمس مائة.

Ahmed : Is there cheap one?

أحمد : فيه أرخص؟

Sajid : Why not? All these are cheap. What is your budget?

ساجد : ليش لا، هذه كلها ساعات رخيصة ميزانيتك كم؟

Ahmed : 300/-

أحمد : ثلاث مائات.

Sajid : Well, come with me. We will go up and see.

ساجد : تعال معي، نرح فوق و نشف.

118

Ahmed : Fine	أحمد : زين.
Sajid : Accurate will do?	ساجد : اكوريت يمشي؟
Ahmed : Let me see it first	أحمد : خلني شف أولا.
Sajid : Accurate watches are cheap and beautiful	ساجد : ساعات أكوريت جميلة ورخيصة.
Ahmed : Howmuch is this?	أحمد : هذه كم؟
Sajid : This I will give you for 150/- Riyal and this purse is free with this. Take two if you want.	ساجد : أعطيك هذه بما ئة وخمسين ريال وهذه المحفظة بلاش مع هذه. خذ إثنين ان تبغ.
Ahmed : OK, give me this	أحمد : زين، أعطني هذه.
Sajid : Do you need invoice?	ساجد : تبغ فاتورة.
Ahmed : No, I don't want. Where should I pay?	أحمد : لا، لا أبغ، وين أدفع؟
Sajid : Go down and pay at the cash	ساجد : رح تحت وادفع عند أمين الصندوق.
Ahmed : Thank you Sajid, I will see you later.	أحمد : شكرا يا ساجد، أشفك بعدين.
Sajid : See you	ساجد : إلى اللقاء.
Ahmed : Have you got change for 500/-	أحمد : عندك قردة لخمس مائة؟
Cashier : Yes	أمين الصندوق : أيوا.
Khalid : Did you go to Sajid? Did you get a watch?	خالد : أنت رحت إلى ساجد، حصلت ساعة.
Ahmed : Look this is the watch.	أحمد : أيوا شف هذه الساعة

119

Khalid : Excellent, for howmuch did you buy this? — خالد : ممتاز، بكم إشتريت هذه؟

Ahmed : Only 150/- Where are you staying now Khalid? — أحمد : مائة وخمسون فقط. وين ساكن الحين أنت يا خالد؟

Khalid : In Najma — خالد : في نجمة.

Ahmed : How do you come here? — أحمد : كيف تجيئ هني؟

Khalid : In taxi — خالد : في تاكسي.

Ahmed : And how do you go home? Can we go together? — أحمد : وكيف ترح بيت؟ ممكن نرح سوا سوا.

Khalid : I will be little late — خالد : أنا متأخر شوي.

Ahmed : No Problem, I have some work in the market — أحمد : ما في مشكلة، عندي شغل في السوق.

Khalid : Could we go at 10 o"Clock — خالد : ممكن نرح الساعة عشرة.

Ahmed : Fine, No problem, I will be there in front of the mosque — أحمد : زين، ما في مشكلة، أكون موجود أمام المسجد.

Khalid : Fine, We shall meet in front of the mosque at 10 O' Clock — خالد : زين، نلتقي أمام المسجد الساعة العاشرة.

Ahmed : Good bye — أحمد : مع السلامة.

Khalid : Good bye — خالد : في أمان الله

6. At the airport *fil matar* — في المطار

Police : Passport Please — شرطة : جواز السفر من فضلك

Babu : Here is my Passport — بابو : ها هو ذا جواز سفري

Police : Where are you coming from?

شرطة : من وين أنت قادم؟

Babu : I'm coming from London

بابو : أنا قادم من لندن

Police : Where is the entry visa?

شرطة : وين تأشيرة الدخول؟

Babu : Here is my Visa

بابو : ها هو ذا تأشيرتي

Police : How long do you want to stay here?

شرطة : كم تبغي ان تبقى هني؟

Babu : Two weeks

بابو : أسبوعين

Police : Have you got anything to declare?

شرطة : هل عندك شيئ للاعلان عنه؟

Babu : No, Nothing

بابو : لا ما في شيئ

Police : Please open this bag

شرطة : من فضلك إفتح هذه الشنطة

Babu : Just a moment

بابو : لحظة شوي

Police : You have to pay duty for this

شرطة : لازم تدفع الرسوم على هذا

Babu : Where can I pay the duty?

بابو : وين أدفع الرسوم؟

Police : There, Have you got any other bags?

شرطة : هناك، هل معك حقائب أخرى؟

Babu : There is a small hand bag

بابو : في شنطة يدوية صغيرة

Police : Take your bag from here

شرطة : خذ حقيبتك من هني

Babu : Where is the porter?

بابو : أين الشيال؟

Police : May be outside

شرطة : ممكن برا

Babu : Where is the car hire office?	بابو : وين مكتب تأجير السيارات؟
Police : Go straight and see it on your right	شرطة : رح سيتا وشف على يمينك
Babu : How can I go to the duty free market?	بابو : كيف أرح إلى سوق الحرة؟
Police : Go up from here	شرطة : رح فوق من هني
Babu : Do you have the map of the country?	بابو : هل عندك خريطة للبلاد؟
Police : Not available with me, see with the hotel's office	شرطة : مش موجود عندي، شف لدى مكتب الفنادق.
Babu : Thanks	بابو : شكرا
Police : Welcome	شرطة : عفوا
Babu : What a surprise, who is this? What do you do here?	بابو : يا للمفاجأة. مين هذا. شو سوي هني؟
Sabu : I was on a short visit, and you?	سابو : كنت في زيارة قصيرة، وأنت؟
Babu : I'm coming from London. I want to learn Arabic	بابو : أنا قادم من لندن، أريد أن أدرس العربية
Sabu : Really! Are you crazy?	سابو : حقا، هل أنت مجنون؟
Babu : Perhaps	بابو : ربما
Sabu : Where do you study Arabic?	سابو : وين تدرس العربية؟
Babu : At the language institute	بابو : في معهد اللغات
Sabu : How about the fee?	سابو : كيف الرسوم؟

Babu : It is free from the Government side	بابو : هذا مجانا من طرف الحكومة
Sabu : I'm in a hurry, Give me your address. I will keep in touch with you in my next visit.	سابو : أنا على عجلة، أعطني عنوانك، سأتصل بك في زيارتي القادمة
Babu : You are welcome. Here is my address	بابو : اهلا بك، خذ هذا عنواني
Sabu : Thanks	سابو : شكرا
Babu : Welcome	بابو : عفوا
Sabu : See you	سابو : إلى اللقاء
Babu : See you	بابو : إلى اللقاء

7. Visiting the neighbour   *ziyarat aljaar*   زيارة الجار

Jabir : Assalamu Alaikum	جابر : السلام عليكم
Jalees : Wa Alaikumussalam wa rahmathullah	جليس : وعليكم السلام ورحمة الله
Jabir : I'm Jabir, your new neighbour	جابر : أنا جابر، جاركم الجديد
Jalees : Most welcome, I'm Jalees	جليس : اهلا وسهلا، وأنا جليس
Jabir : Is this your son?	جابر : هل هذا إبنك؟
Jalees : Yes, this is my son	جليس : نعم هذا إبني
Jabir : What is his name?	جابر : شسمه؟
Jalees : Hamza	جليس : حمزة
Jabir : How old is he?	جابر : كم عمره؟
Jalees : Four years	جليس : أربع سنوات
Jabir : Is this your daughter?	جابر : وهل هذه إبنتك؟

123

Jalees : Yes, this is my daughter

جليس : نعم هذه إبنتي

Jabir : How old is she?

جابر : كم عمرها؟

Jalees : Seven years, this is your house, please come

جليس : سبع سنوات، تفضل هذا بيتك

Jabir : Thanks, I will visit you shortly Insha Allah

جابر : شكرا، سأزورك قريبا إن شاء الله

Jalees : Good bye

جليس : مع السلامة

Jabir : See you

جابر : الى اللقاء

Hamid : Calling bell is ringing

حامد : جرس البيت يرن

Jalees : Open the door, son!

جليس : إفتح الباب يا بني

Hamid : This is our neighbour Jabir and his family

حامد : هذا جارنا جابر وأسرته

Jabir : Good evening

جابر : مساء الخير

Jalees : Good evening, most welcome

جليس : مساء النور، اهلا وسهلا

Jabir : This is my wife Abida, and this is my son Jassim

جابر : هذه زوجتي عابدة، وهذا إبني جاسم

Jalees : And who is this?

جليس : ومن هذه؟

Jabir : And this is my daughter Ruqiyya

جابر : وهذه إبنتي رقية

Jalees : Welcome, How are you?

جليس : مرحبا، كيف حالكم؟

Jabir : Good, praise be to Allah

جابر : بخير، الحمد لله

Jalees : Please come to the sitting room

جليس : فضلو إلى غرفة الجلوس

Jabir : Thanks

جابر : شكرا

124

Jalees : This is my wife Rasheeda, and this is my son Mubarak

جليس : هذه زوجتي رشيدة، وهذا إبني مبارك

Jabir : And who is this?

جابر : ومن هذه؟

Jalees : And this is my daughter Hamda

جليس : وهذه إبنتي حمدة

Jabir : How many rooms are there in the house?

جابر : كم غرفة في البيت

Jalees : Five rooms, This is the sitting room and that is the dining room. Bed rooms are there

جليس : خمس غرف، هذه غرفة الجلوس وتلك غرفة الطعام وهناك غرفة النوم

Jabir : How much is the rent?

جابر: إجار كم؟

Jalees : 3000/- Riyals per month

جليس : ٣٠٠٠ ريال شهريا

Jabir : Water and electricity are free or not?

جابر: الكهرباء والماء مجانا، أم لا؟

Jalees : Nothing is free, We must pay everything

جليس : ما في شيئ مجانا لازم ندفع كله

Jabir : How much does it come monthly?

جابر : كم يأتي شهريا في هذا؟

Jalees : Around 300/- Riyals

جليس : ٣٠٠ ريال تقريبا

Jalees : What would you like to drink Tea or Pepsi?

جليس : شن تشربون، شاي أو ببسي؟

Jabir : We prefer tea

جابر : نفضل الشاي

Jalees : With milk or without milk?

جليس : بالحليب أو بدون حليب

Jabir : Without milk is better

جابر : بدون حليب أحسن

Jalees : What about sugar?

جليس: سكر كيف؟

Jabir : Normal	جابر : عادي
Jalees : Mubarak! Bring tea for all	جليس : يا مبارك، جب شاي للجميع
Mubarak : Please help yourself	مبارك : فضلوا
Jabir : May Allah reward you nicely, When will you visit us?	جابر : جزاك الله خيرا، ومتى تزوروننا؟
Jalees : Next Friday, Insha Allah	جليس : في الجمعة القادمة إن شاء الله
Jabir : Please excuse us now. We have guests for dinner today	جابر : نعتذر الحين، لنا ضيوف للعشاء اليوم
Jalees : No problem, It was a happy occasion	جليس : ما ليش، مناسبة سعيدة
Jabir : I will see you on Friday. Good bye	جابر : أشوفكم الجمعة، مع السلامة
Jalees : Good bye	جليس : في أمان الله

8. At the street *fi shshari'h* في الشارع

Habeeb : Good morning	حبيب : صباح الخير
Khalid : Good morning	خالد : صباح النور
Habeeb : How are you?	حبيب : كيف حالك؟
Khalid : Fine, Praise be to Allah, and you?	خالد : بخير، الحمد لله وأنت؟
Habeeb : Good, Praise be to Allah	حبيب : طيب، والحمد لله
Khalid : Where are you from Habeeb?	خالد : من وين إنت يا حبيب؟
Habeeb : I'm from India	حبيب : أنا من الهند
Khalid : Where in India?	خالد : وين في الهند؟
Habeeb : In Kerala	حبيب : في كيرلا

Khalid : How long are you in Doha?	خالد : كم سنة أنت في الدوحة؟
Habeeb : Five years, and you?	حبيب : خمس سنوات، وأنت؟
Khalid : I'm born in Doha	خالد : أنا مولود بالدوحة
Habeeb : Where do you work Khalid?	حبيب : وين تشتغل يا خالد؟
Khalid : I'm working with Q tel, and what do you do Habeeb?	خالد : أشتغل في كيوتل، وشسوي يا حبيب؟
Habeeb : I have a grocery in the market	حبيب : عندي بقالة في السوق
Khalid : How's the business?	خالد : كيف التجارة؟
Habeeb : Going on	حبيب : يمشي
Khalid : Where are you going now?	خالد : وين رح الحين؟
Habeeb : I'm going to the vegetable market	حبيب : أرح إلى سوق الخضر
Khalid : How do you go? Have you got a car?	خالد : كيف ترح؟ عندك سيارة؟
Habeeb : I will go with my friend. I'm waiting from him	حبيب : أرح مع صديقي، أنا في إنتظاره
Khalid : What time will you return from the market?	خالد : ساعة كم رجع من السوق؟
Habeeb : After two hours Insha Allah	حبيب : بعد ساعتين، إن شاء الله
Khalid : Here is my friend coming, I'm going with him	خالد : ها هو ذا صديقي يجئ، أرح معه
Habeeb : Good bye	حبيب : مع السلامة
Khalid : See you	خالد : إلى اللقاء

9. In the class room

fi ssaf   في الصف

Hamid : Where is your book Ahmed?	حامد: وين كتابك يا أحمد؟
Ahmed : I don't know, May be at home	أحمد: ما أدري، ممكن في البيت
Hamid : Why didn't you bring the book?	حامد: ليش لم تأتي بالكتاب؟
Ahmed : I forgot it dear	أحمد: نسيته يا حبيبي
Hamid : How do you study without book?	حامد: كيف تدرس بدون كتاب؟
Ahmed: I will write in the note book	أحمد: أكتب في دفتر
Hamid : Don't repeat this I will tell your father	حامد: لا تكرر هذا أقل بابا
Ahmed : Did you complete the home work?	أحمد: خلصت الواجب؟
Hamid : I completed it yesterday	حامد: خلصته أمس
Ahmed : Come on, let us play foot ball today	أحمد: هيا، نلعب كرة اليوم
Hamid : No, I would like to play basket ball	حامد: لا، أبغ ألعب كرة السلة
Ahmed : Come fast, the time is short	أحمد: زين تعال سرعة، الوقت قصير
Hamid : Come on, let us go	حامد: هيا، نرح
Ahmed : Come on	أحمد: هيا

10. At home   *fil bayti*   في البيت

Rafeek : Assalamu Alaikum

رفيق: السلام عليكم

Salman : Wa Alaikumussalam

سلمان: وعليكم السلام

Rafeek : Where were you
yesterday?

رفيق: وين كنت با لأمس؟

Salman : I was in our uncle
Abdulla's house

سلمان: كنت في بيت عمنا عبد
الله

Rafeek : How are the
children of uncle?

رفيق:كيف أولاد العم؟

Salman : All are fine, and
praise be to Allah

سلمان: كلهم طيبون، والحمد لله

Rafeek : Where are you going today?

رفيق: وين ترح اليوم؟

Salman : I'm going to the
house of our Aunt. I heard
she is sick

سلمان: أرح بيت خالتنا، سمعت
أها مريضة

Rafeek : What time you will go?

رفيق: ساعة كم ترح؟

Salman : At 10 AM

سلمان: الساعة عاشرة صباحا

Rafeek : How do you go?

رفيق: كيف ترح؟

Salman : By bus

سلمان: في الباص

Rafeek : Who with you go?

رفيق: مع مين ترح؟

Salman : Me alone

سلمان: وحدي

Rafeek : It can not be, Go
with your elder brother

رفيق: هذا لا يسير، رح مع أخيك
الكبير

Salman : My brother has
examination tomorrow and
he is very busy

سلمان : أخي له إمتحان بكرة،
هو مشغول واجد

Rafeek : Come fast, I will drop you.

رفيق: تعال سرعة، أنا ودعــك

Salman : OK. I will come now

سلمان: زين، أتي الحين

Rafeek : When will you return from the Aunt's house?

رفيق: متى ترجع من بيت الخالة؟

Salman : Day after tomorrow, Insha Allah

سلمان: بعد بكرة، إن شاء الله

Rafeek : OK. You call me, I will send a car to you

رفيق: زين، إتصل بي، أرسل لك سيارة

Salman : Thank you so much

سلمان: شكرا جزيلا

Rafeek : Come on, let us go, the time is late

رفيق: هيا، نرح، الوقت متأخر

Salman : I'm ready, let us go

سلمان: أنا جاهز، هيا نرح

Rafeek : We have reached the house of Aunt, get down

رفيق: ها قد وصلنا بيت الخالة، أنزل

Salman : Good bye

سلمان: مع السلامة

Rafeek : Good bye

رفيق: في أمان الله

LESSON NINETEEN

SOME QUESTIONS

1. What is your name?	۱) شسمك؟
2. Where are you from?	۲) من وين أنت؟
3. How are you?	۳) كيف الحال؟ / كيفك؟ / شلونك؟ / شخبارك؟ / ماشي الحال؟
4. How old are you?	٤) كم عمرك؟
5. Where are you residing?	٥) أنت ساكن وين؟
6. Where are your children?	٦) وين أولادك؟
7. Where do you work?	٧) وين تشتغل؟
8. Where is your office?	٨) وين مكتبك؟
9. Where are you going?	٩) وين ترح؟ / وين رح؟
10. What you want?	۱۰. ايش تبغ؟ / شن تبغ؟ / ايش تريد؟ / شن تريد؟
11. How do you go home?	۱۱) كيف ترح بيت؟
12. What is the problem?	۱۲) شن فيه؟ / ايش فيه؟
13. Have you got a car?	۱۳) عندك سيارة؟
14. Who is this?	۱٤) مين هذا؟
15. How is he?	۱٥) كيف هو؟
16. Whose car is this?	۱٦) سيارة مين هذه
17. Whom do you want?	۱۷) مين تبغ؟

18. Which market you go to?   ١٨) أي سوق ترح؟

19. Howmany days you want?   ١٩) كم يوما تبغ؟

20. How much you will give me?   ٢٠) كم تعطني؟

21. Whose duty is tomorrow?   ٢١) دوام من بكرة؟

22. Who made a call?   ٢٢) من سوي تلفون؟

23. Can I speak to the manager? ٢٣) ممكن كلم المدير؟

24. When will he come?   ٢٤) متى يجيئ

25. Why didn't you come yesterday? ٢٥) ليش لم تجي بالأمس؟

LESSON TWENTY

VOCABULARY

Here I would like to give you a selected list of words which I feel will help you to interact in good language, provided you do the course systematically and on a consistent basis. The importance of a dictionary in a spoken language book is that it will serve as a guide to the beginner to form his questions and answers required for the interactive practices. I do not claim this as a full proofed dictionary, but present as a preferred list of words to those who wish to improve their spoken skills in the language.

A

A	واحد	Active	نشيط
A lot of	كمية كبيرة من	Actor	ممثل
A. M.	قبل الظهــــر	Actually	في الواقع، فعلا
Able to	ممكن	Adapt (to)	يوفق بين، يكيف
About	عن حوالي	Adapter	محول
Above	فوق	Add	يضيف
Accept	قبل	Add(to)	يضيف
Accident	حادثة	Adding	مضيفا
Account	حساب	Addition	الجمع
Accountant	محاسب	Addition	زيادة
Ache	ألم	Address book	دفتر عناوين
Across	عبر	Address	عنوان
Act (to)	يمثل مسرحيا	Adjective	صفة
Act	فصل من مسرحية	Administration manager	مدير الإدارة
		Admire(to)	يعجب، يستحسن

Admission	دخول	Airport	مطار
Adore(to)	يعبد، يعشق	Alcohol	كحول
Adult	كبير	Alike	شبيه ، مثيل
Adventure	مغامرة	All over	في كل مكان
Adverb	ظرف	All about	كل ما يتعلق ب
Adverbial	ظرفي	All around	في كل مكان
Advertisement	إعلان	All right	وهو كذلك
Advisor	واعظ	All	كل، جميع
Advocate	محامي	Allergy	حساسية
Affirmative	إثبات	Almost	تقريبا
Afraid	يخاف	Alone	وحيد
Afraid(to be)	يخاف، يكون خائفا	Along	على الطول، امتداد
After a while	بعد قليل	Alphabet	حروف
After all	ومع ذلك	Already	فعلا
After	بعد	Also	أيضا
Afternoon	بعد الظهر، الأصيل	Although	رغم أن
Again	أيضا، مرة أخرى	Always	دائما
Against	ضد	Ambassador	سفير
Age	عمر	Ambulance	سيارة إسعاف
Agency	وكالة	Among	بين(أكثر من اثنين)
Agent	وكيل	Amount	مبلغ
Ago	من مدة، قبل	Amplifier	مكبر صوت/ سماعة
Agree (to)	يوافق، يتفق مع	An	واحد، واحدة
Agreement	اتفاقية	Analgesic	مسكن
Ahead	أمام، قدام	Ancient	قديم
Air hostess	مضيفة	And	و
Air port	مطار، ميناء جوى	Anesthetic	مخدر
Air	الهواء	Angry	غضبان
Airmail	بريد جوي	Animal	حيوان
Airplane	طائرة	Annual	سنوي

Another	آخر	Asleep	نائم
Answer	إجابة	Assistant	مساعد
Answer(to)	يجيب	At all	بالمرة، إطلاقا
Ant	نملة	At ease	على راحتك
Anxious	قلق	At Least	على الأقل
Anxiously	بقلق، بشوق	At once	فورا
Any more	غير ذلك، بعد ذلك	At	عند
Any where	أي مكان	Athlete	رياضي
Any	أية، أي (فقط للاستفهام والنفي)	Attract(to)	يجذب، يغرى
Anybody	أي شخص	Attractive	جذاب، مغرى
Anyone	أي شخص	Aunt	العمة أو الخالة
Anything	أي شئ	Author	مؤلف
Apple	تفاحة	Authorise	وكل
Apron	مئزر، مريلة(للمطبخ)	Autumn	خريف
Architect	مهندس معماري	Auxiliary	مساعد
Are	يكو نون، تكونون، يكنّ	Awake	مستيقظ ، متيقظ
Area	منطقة	Awake(to)-	يستيقظ
Arm	ذراع	Away	بعيد
Armchair	كرسي ذو ذراعين	Awful	شديد ،فظيع ،مخيف
Armed force	قوات المسلحة	**B**	
Around	حول	Baby sitter	حارسة أطفال
Arrival	وصول	Baby	طفل/ رضيع
Arrive(to)	يصل	Bachelor	عازب
Art	فن	Back	ظهر/خلف
Article	حرف جر	Bad	سيئ
Artificial	صناعي	Badly	بطريقة سيئة ، بطرقة رديئة
Artist	رسام	Bag	حقيبة ، كيس ، زكيبة
Artist	فنان	Bake(to)	يخبز
Artiste	فنان	Baker	خباز
Ask (to)	يسال	Bakery	مخبز

Balcony	شرفة	Before	قبل
Ball	كرة	Began	بدأ
Balloon	بالون	Begin(to)began-begun	يبدأ
Banana	موز	Beginning	بداية
Bandage	رباط	Behave(to)	يتصرف / يسلك
Bank	ضفة نهر ، بنك ، مصرف	Behind	وراء
Barber	حلاق	Believe, believe(to)	يؤمن ، يعتقد
Bark(to)	ينبح		
Barker	فرامل	Bell	جرس
Baron	بارون	Belong (to)	ينتمي إلى
Basket	سلة	Below	تحت
Basket-ball	كرة السلة	Belt	حزام
Bath(to)	يستحم	Bench	مقعد
Bathroom	حمام	Beside	بجانب
Battle	معركة	Besides	عدا ، علاوة على
Bay	خليج	Best	الأحسن (مقارن بين أكثر من أثنين)
Bazaar	سوق		
BC.(before Christ)	قبل الميلاد	Better	احسن من
Be(to)-was-been	يكون،يوجد	Between	بين
Beach	شاطئ	Bicycle	دراجة
Beak	منقار	Big	كبير
Bear	دب	Bin	علبة القمامة
Beard	ذقن ، لحية	Biology	علم الأحياء
Beat(to)	يهزم (في مباراة) يضرب	Bird	طير
Beautiful	جميل	Birdie	طائرة صغير
Because	لأن	Birth	ميلاد
Bed	سرير	Birthday	عيد ميلاد
Bedroom	حجرة النوم	Bitch	أنثى الكلب
Bee	نحلة	Bite(to)bit-bitten-bit	يعض
Beef	لحم البقرة	Bitter	مر

Black smith	حداد	Bracket	قوس
Black	اسود	Brain	مخ
Blackboard	سبورة	Brake	كسر
Blade	موس	Branch	فرع شجرة
Blank	فراغ	Break down	عطل
Blind	أعمى، كفيف، فاقد	Break fast	الفطور
Blood pressure	ضغط الدم	Break	استراحة قصيرة
Blood Transfusion	نقل الدم	Breast	ثدي
Blood	دم	Breath	تنفس
Blow (to) – blew – blown	يعب	Bridge	جسر
Blue	ازرق	Bright	لامع ، براق
Board	لوحة	Brightly	بطريقة براقة ــ بلمعان
Boarder	حدود	Bring (to)- brought	يحضر، يجلب
Boat	مركب	Bring	احضر
Body	جسم	Broken	مكسور
Bone	عظم	Brother	أخ
Book shop	مكتبة	Brother-in-law	أخو الزوج ، أخو الزوجة
Book	كتاب		
Booking office	مكتب حجز	Brown	بني
Born (to be)	يولد	Brush	فرشاة ، فرجون
Borrow (to)	يستعير، يقترض، يستلف	Brush(to)	فرش ، نفض الغبار
		Bucket	دلو ، جردل
Both	كلا	Build(to)-built-	يبني
Bottle	رجاجة	Builder	بناء
Bottom	تحت	Building	مبنى
Boundary	حدود	Bull	ثور
Box (to)	يلاكم	Burn	حرق
Box	صندوق	Bury(to)-buried-	يدفن
Boy	ولد		

Bus	حافلة
Bush	شجيرة
Business	تجارة
Business	عمل، شغل، أعمال
Bus-stop	موقف حافلة
Busy	مشغول
But	لكن
Butcher	جزار
Butter	زبد
Butterfly, butterflies	فراشة، فراشات
Button	زرار
Buy	اشترى
Buzz	طنين ــ أزير
By	بواسطة ، قريباً
Bye	وداعا (مختصرة)

C

Cabin-cruiser	يخت صغير
Cage	قفص
Cake	كعكة
Calculator	آلة حاسبة
Calendar	تقويم
Call off(to)	يلغي ، يوقف
Call	سمي
Call	مكالمة
Call(to)	ينادي ــ يسمى ، يدعو
Calm	هادئ
Camel	جمل
Camp	عسكر

Can	ممكن
Cancel	ألغي
Can-could	يقدر
Candle	شمعة
Cape	رأس ــ أرض داخلة في البحر
Capital	رأس مال / عاصمة
Captain	قبطان ــ رئيس
Car hire	تأجير سيارات
Car park	موقف سيارات
Car	سيارة
Cardinal	الأرقام الأصلية
Cards	ورق لعب
Care(to)	يهتم ب ــ يبالي ب
Careful	حذر
Carefully	بعناية
Careless	مهمل
Carpenter	نجار
Carpet	سجادة
Carrot	جزر
Carry(to)-carried-	يحمل ، ينقل
Case / box	علبة
Case	حالة
Cashier	أمين صندوق
Cat	قط ، قطة
Catch(to)-caught-	يمسك
Caution	احترس
Ceiling	سقف
Celebrate(to)	يحتفل ب
Celebration	احتفال

138

VOCABULARY

Censor	مراقب	Circle	دائرة
Censoring	مراقبة	Circular / notice	تعميم
Centre	مركز	City-state	مدينة ــ مدن
Centre	وسط	Classmate	رفيق الصف ، زميل
Century	قرن		الدراسة ، زميلة الدراسة
Certainly	يقينا ، بكل تأكيد	classroom	فصل في مدرسة
Certificate	شهادة	Claw	مخلب (حيوان أو طائر)
Chain	سلسلة	Clean (to)	ينظف
Chair	كرسي	Clean	نظيف
Change	بدل	Clerk	كاتب
Change(to)	يغير	Clever	ذكي
Chase	يطارد	Climate	مناخ
Chat	حديث	Climb (to)	يسلق ، يطلع ، يصعد
Cheap	رخيص	Climber	متسلق
Cheat(to)	يخدع ، يغش	Clinic	عيادة
Check in	تسجيل	Clock	ساعة
Check to	كشف	Close	قفل / قريب
Cheek	خد ، وجنة	Clothes	قماش / أقمشة
Cheese	جبن	Cloud	سحابة
Cheque	حوالة	Cloudy	مغيم، غائم ، كثي
Cherry, cherries	الكرز	Club	نادي
Chick	فرخ ، كتكوت	Coach	مدرب
Chief	رئيس	Coast	ساحل البحر
Child, children	طفل ، أطفال	Coat	معطف
Chimney	مدخلة	Cock	ديك
Chirp (to)	يصدح ، يزقزق ــ يغرد	Coffee	قهوة
Choice	اختيار	Coffee-pot	ركوة قهوة، تنكة قهوة
Choose (to) chose-chosen	يختار	Coin/currency	عملة
Church	كنيسة	Cold	بارد
Cigar	سيجار	Cold	زكام
		Collar	ياقة

Collide (to)	يتصادم ، يصطدم	Constipation	إمساك
Color	لون	Consultant	مستشاري
Column	عمود ، نصب	Contagious	معدي
Come back	يعود	Contain (to)	يحتوي على
Come (to) –came	يحضر	Contents	محتويات
Come down(to)	ينزل	Continent	قارة
Come in(to)	يدخل	Continue (to)	يستمر
Come on	هيا	Continuous	مستمر
Come out (to)	يخرج	Contraception	عازل
Come	آتي	Contract	عقد
Comedy	ملهاة	Contracted form	الشكل المختصر
Comfortable	مريحة	Contractor	مقاول
Commission	عمولة	Conversation	محادثة
Comp	مشط	Cook (to)	يطبخ ، يطهو
Companion	رفيق ، صاحب	Cook	طباخ
Company	صحبة ، رفقة	Cool	رطب ، بارد باعتدال
Comparative degree	درجة المقارنة بين أثنين	Copy book	كراسة
Comparison	مقارنة	Copy	نسخة
Competition	مناقشة/ منافسة	Corn	ذرة
Complaint	شكوى	Corner	ركن
Complete (to)	يكمل	Correct (to)	يصحح
Composition	تعبير ، إنشاء	Correct	صحيح
Compulsory	مجبور	Correction	تصحيح ، تصويب
Concert	حفلة موسيقية	Corresponding	مناظر ، مطابق
Conductor	قائد فرقة	Cost (to)-cost-	يتكلف ، يساوي
Confirm	أكد	Cost	سعر
Confirmation	تأكيد	Count (to)	يعد
Conflict	مجادلة	Countable	قابل للعد
Congratulation	تهاني	Country, countries	بلد، قطر، أقطار
Connection	مواصلة	Cousin	ابن أو بنت العمة أو العم

VOCABULARY

Cover	غطاء
Cow	بقرة
Crave (to)	يشتاق
Creature	مخلوق
Credit (on)	بطريق القرض
Credit	رصيد
Creep (to) –crept-	يزحف
Cross (to)	يعبر
Cross	صليب
Crow	غراب
Crowd	زحام ، حشد
Crowded	مزدحم بالناس
Cry (to)-cried-	يزعق ، يصرخ
Cucumber	خيار
Cup	فنجان
Curious	عجيب ، غريب
Curtain	ستارة
Custom	عادة
Cut (to	يقطع
Cut of service	انقطاع الخدمة

D

Dad	أب ، بابا
Daily	يومي
Dance	رقصة
Dance(to)	يرقص
Dangerous	خطير
Dark	ظلام
Darkness	ظلمة
Darling	عزيز،حبيب،محبوب

Date	تاريخ
Date	تمر
Daughter – in–law	زوجة الابن
Daughter	ابنة
Dawn	فجر ، سحر
Day	نهار
Day	يوم
Days of the week	أيام الأسبوع
Dead	ميت
Dear	عزيز
Death	موت، وفاة
Debt	دين
Decide(to)	يقرر، يعقد العزم
Decision	قرار
Declare	أعلن
Decorate (to)	بزين ، يزخرف
Deep (the)	عميق (الماء)
Defeat(to)	يهزم
Defective	معيب ، ناقص
Definite article	أداة تعريف
Degree	درجة (ترمومتر)
Degrees of comparison	درجات المقارنة
Delay	تأخير
Delicious	لذيذ
Deliver (to)	يسلم ، يوزع
Deliver	وصل
Democracy	ديمقراطية
Dentist	طبيب أسنان

Denture	طقم
Department	قسم
Departure	مغادرة / رحيل
Deposit	ضمان
Describe (to)	يصف
Describe	وصف
Description	وصف
Desert	صحراء
Destination	اتجاه، جهة الوصول
Details of calls	تفاصيل المكالمات
Develop	حمض
Diabetic	السكر
Dial to	اتصل
Dialogue	حوار
Diamond	ماسة
Diarrhea	إسهال
Diary, diaries	يومية، مفكرة، يوميات، مفكرات
Dictionary	قاموس
Did	فعل (مع كل الضمائر)
Die (to)	يموت ، يحتضر
Difference	اختلاف
Different	مختلف
Difficult	صعب
Difficulty	صعوبة
Dig (to)-dug-	يعزق ، يحفر
Dine (to)	يتناول العشاء
Dining –room	حجرة الطعام
Dinner	عشاء
Direct	مباشر
Direction	اتجاه / جهة
Director	مدير
Directory	دليل
Dirt/ dirty	قذر / قذارة
Disable	عاجز
Discount	خصم
Discover(to)	يكتشف
Discovery	اكتشاف
Disease	مرض
Dish	أكلة
Distance	مسافة
District	ناحية ، مقاطعة
Divide (to)	يقسم
Division	قسمة
Doctor	دكتور / طبيب
Donkey	حمار
Down	تحت
Dozen	دستة
Dress maker	خياط
Dress	فستان
Drink	شرب
Drive	ساق
Driver	سواق
Dry	جاف
Duck	بط
Dummy	بذارة
During	أثناء
Duty free	سوق الحرة

Duty	رسوم
Dye	صبغة
Dyer	صباغ

E

East	شرق
Editor in chief	رئيس التحرير
Egg	بيضة
Elastic	مطاط
Electric	كهربائي
Elevator	مصعد
Email	بريد إلكتروني
Embassy	سفارة
Emergency exit	مخرج طوارئ
Emergency	طوارئ
Emir	أمير
Empty	فاضي
End	آخر
Engineer	مهندس
Enjoy	عجب
Enlarge	كبر
Enough	يكفي
Enquirey	استعلامات
Entry	دخول
Envelope	ظرف
Equipment	أدوات
Eraser	ممحاة
Estimate	سعر تقريبي
Evening	مساء
Every month	كل شهر
Every week	كل أسبوع
Every year	كل سنة

Everything	كل شيء
Examine	فحص
Exchange	بدالة
Excursion	جوالة سياحية
Excuse	عفو / سماح
Executive manager	مدير التنفيذي
Exhibition	معرض
Exit	خروج
Expect	انتظر
Expenses	مصاريف
Express	اظهر
External	خارج
Extra	زيادة
Eye	عين

F

Fabrics	قماش
Face	وجه
Factory	مصنع
Fall	سقط
Fall(to)-fell-fallen	يقع، يسقط
Falls	شلالات
Family	أسرة، عائلة
Famous	مشهور
Fan	مروحة
Fantastic	خيالي
Far	بعيد، بعيد عن
Fare	ثمن
Fares	أجرة السفر
Farm	مزرع
Farmer	فلاح

Fast	سريع ، بسرعة	Find	وجد
Fat	دهن	Find(to)-fought-	يجد
Fat	سمين	Fine arts	الفنون الجميلة
Father	والد/ أب	Fine	كويس
Father-in-law	حم	Fine	لطيف،مليح،رقيق،ناعم
Fault	عيب ، خطأ	Finger	اصبح يد
Favourite	مفضل	Finish (to)	ينهى
Fear	خوف	Finish	انتهى
Fear(in)	خائفا	Fire	حريق ، نار
Fee	رسوم	First	أول
Feed(to)-fed-	يطعم	Fish	سمك
Feel	شعر	Fishing	صيد السمك
Feel(to)-felt-	يشعر	Fishing-rod	بوصة صيد
Feet(foot)	أقدام(قدم)	Fishmonger	سماك، تاجر السمك
Fellow	شخص، إنسان	Fit(to)-fitted	يناسب، يلائم
Fever	حمى/ حرارة	Fix	صلح
Few	عدد أقل من القليل	Flag	علم
Few(a)	قليل	Flat	شقة
Field	حقل	Fleet	أسطول
Fig	تين	Flight	طيران،رحلة طيران
Fight	قتال	Floor	طبق،دور، أرضية
Fight(to)-	يعارك،يحارب،	Flour	طابق
fought-	يقاتل	Flow	سائل
Fighter	مجاهد	Flow(to)	يجرى
Fighting	مصارعة	Flower	زهرة
File	ملف	Fly(to)-flew-flown	يطير
Fill	ملأ	Fly, flies	ذبابة ذباب
Fill(to)	يملأ	Follow(to)	يتبع
Finally	أخيرا، في النهاية	Following	التالي

Food	طعام
Fool	أحمق، غبي
Foot ball	كرة القدم
Footballer	لاعب كرة قدم
For instance	على سبيل المثال،مثلا
For	ل ،من أجل
Foreign	أجنبي
Forest	غابة
Forget	نسي
Forget(to)-forgot-forgotten	ينسى
Fork	شوكة
Form	استمارة
Form	شكل،صيغة،قالب
Fort	حصن
Fortunately	الحظ
Fountain	نافورة
Frame	شنبر
Free	خالي
Free	مجانا
Fresh	طازج
Friday	يوم الجمعة
Fried	مقلي
Friend	رفيق/ زميل/ صديق
From	من
Front	أمام
Fruit salad	سلطة فواكه
Fruit	فاكهة
Full	مليان

G

Game	لعبة
Garden	حديقة
Garlic	ثوم
Garment	ملبس
Gate / door	باب
General manager	مدير العام
General telegram office	المكتب العام للبرقيات
General	عام
Genuine	طبيعي
Get off	نزل
Get up	نهض
Girl	بنت
Give me	اعطني
Give	أعطى
Glass	زجاج
Glue	صمغ
Go away	مشى
Go out	خرج
Go	ذهب
Gold	ذهب
Golden	ذهبي
Good by	مع السلامة
Good	جيد
Goods	بضائع
Grand father	جد
Grand mother	جدة
Grape	عنب
Gray	رمادي
Great	عظيم

Green	اخضر	Headache	صداع
Greetings	تحية	Headmaster	ناظر
Grilled	مشوي	Health	صحة
Group	مجموعة	Healthy	صحي
Guide	مرشد	Heavy	ثقيل
Gulf	خليج	Heel	كعب
Gum	لثة	Height	ارتفاع
		Heir	وريث

H

Hair	شعر (جمع)	Heiress	وريثة
Hairdresser's shop	محل حلاقة	Hello	أهلا، هالوا
Half	نصف	Help	نجدة/مساعدة
Hammer	مطرقة	Helper	مساعد
Hand kerchief	منديل	Her	ها (صفة ملكية مفرد
Hand	يد		غائب مؤنث)
Hand(of the clock)	عقرب الساعة	Herbs	أعشاب
Handsome	وسيم	Here	هنا
Hang (to)-hanged-	يعلق (شيئا)	Hero	بطل
Hang (to)-hung-	يعلق ، يشنق	Herself	نفسها
Happen(to)	يحدث	High	عالي
Happily	بسعادة ، بابتهاج	Hill	تل
Happy	سعيد ، مبهج	Himself	نفسه
Hard	صلب ، عسر	Hire	تأجير
Has L have	يملك	History	تاريخ
Hat	قبعة	Hold(to)-held-	يمسك
Hate (to)	يكره	Hole	ثقب
Have(to)-had-had	على أن ، يجب أن	Holiday	إجازة
He	هو	Holy	مقدس
Head	رأس	Home	منزل
		Homework	الواجب المدرسي الذي يتم بالبيت

146

VOCABULARY

Honest	أمين ، صريح	Idiom	عبارة اصطلاحية
Honey	عسل	If	إذا / إن
Hope	تمنى	Ill	مريض
Horse	حصان	Import	مستورد
Horseback (to go on)	صهوة جواد	Important	مهم
		Impossible	غير ممكن
Hospital	مستشفى	In a way	بطريقة ما ، نوعا ما
Hot	ساخن	In all	جملة ، في المجموع
Hotel	فندق	In fear	خائفا
Hour	ساعة	In front of / behind	أمام / وراء
Housewife	ربة البيت		
Housework	أعمال منزلية	In	في
How about	ما رأيك في	Inches	بوصات
How come	كيف يحدث	Included	محسوب
How far	كم المسافة	Incoming	داخل
How long	كم من الوقت	Indeed	حقا
How many	كم	Indoors	داخل المبنى
How much	كم (كمية)	Industrial are:	منطقة الصناعية
How	كيف	Infant	طفل ، رضيع
Huge	ضخم	Infected	ملوث
Hundreds	مئات	Infinitive	مصدر الفعل
Hungry	جوعان	Inflammation	التهاب
Hunt (to)	يصيد ، صائد	Inflation	تضخم
Hunt	صيد	Information	استعلامات
Hunter	صياد ــ صائد	Inhabitant	ساكن، قاطن، مقيم
Hurdle	عائق ، عقبة ، مانع	Injection	حقن
I		Injury	إصابة/ جراح
I	أنا	Ink	حبر
Idea	فكرة	Inn	استراحة

147

Inquiry	استعلامات
insect	حشرة
Inside	داخل
Inspection	تفتيش
Inspector	مفتش
Instead	بدلا من
Instruction	تعليمية ، أمر
Insurance	تامين
Interest	فائدة
Interested	اهتم
Interesting	ممتع (صفة)
International	دولي
International call	مكالمة خارجية
Interpreter / translator	مترجم
Interrogative	استفهامي
Interview	مقابلة
Into	داخل (عادة مصحوبة بحركة)
Introduce	قدم
Introduction	تقديم / تعارف
Invent(to)	يخترع
Inventor	مخترع
Investment	استثمار
Invitation	دعوة
Invite (to)	يدعو
Invoice	فاتورة
Iron	كوى
Irregular	غير قياسي
Island	جزيرة
It	هو، هي (غير عاقل)

J

Jam	ازدحام ، حشد
Jar	برطمان (للمربي)
Jet	طائرة نفاثة
Jewel	جوهرة
Jewelry	مجوهرات
Job	عمل ، شغل
Joint	مفصل
Journalist	صحافي
Journey	رحلة
Joy	فرح ، سرور
Judge	حاكم
Jug	قدر ، إبريق
Juice	عصير
Jump(to)	يقفز
Just	فقط

K

Keep (to)- kept-	يحفظ ، يحتفظ ب
Keep quiet(to)	يلتزم الصمت ، يلزم السكوت
Keep	حفظ
Kettle	غلاية
Key	مفتاح
Kick(to)	رفس ــ يركل ، رفسة
Kidney	كلى
Kill(to)	يقتل
Kind	صنف/ نوع
Kind	لطيف
King	ملك
Kiss	يقبل

Kitchen	مطبخ	Lawn مرجوة ــ قطعة أرض خضراء	
Kite	طائرة ورقية	Lay(to)-laid- يضع، يركن، يبيض	
Kits	اختصار	Lay(to)the يرتب المنضدة ،	
Knee	ركبة	table يعد المائدة	
Knife, knives	سكين ، سكاكين	Lazy	كسول
Knock(to)	يقرع ، يدق ، يطرق	Leader	زعيم / امام
Know	عرف	Leaf, leaves ورقة شجر ،	
Know(to)-knew-known	يعرف ، يعلم	أوراق شجر	
		Leap(to)	يقفز
L		Learn(to)	يتعلم
Lab technician	فني مختبر	Learned	متعلم
Laboratory	مختبر	Least	الأقل
Ladder	سلم	Leather	جلد
Lady, ladies	السيدة ، السيدات	Leave إجازة ــ عطلة	
Lake	بحيرة	Leave(to)-left- يترك ، يرحل	
Lamd	أرض ــ بر	Left	شمال
Land	قمبط الطائرة	Left	يسار
Landlord	صاحب البيت	Leg	ساق
Landscape	منظر	Leg ساق ــ رجل (للكرسي مثلا)	
Language	لغة	Lend(to)-lent يعير ، يسلف	
Large	كبير	Length	طول
Last	أخير	Lens	عدسة
Late	متأخر	Less	اقل
Laugh	ضحك	Lesson	درس
Laugh(to)	يضحك	Letter حرف، رسالة، خطاب	
Launching	تدشين	Lettuce	خس
Laundry	مغسلة	License	رخصة
Law	قانون	Lie(to)-lay-lain	يكذب
		Lie(to)lied-	يرقد
		Life	حياة

Lift	مصعد	Long	طويل
Light	خفيف	Look at (to)	ينظر إلى
Light	ضوء	Look down (to)	ينظر إلى أسفل
Light(to)-lit-	يشعل	Look for	بحث عن
Like	كما ، مثل ، كأن	Look like (to)	يشبه
Like(to)	يحب	Look out (to)	يحذر ، ينتبه
Line	خط/ سطر	Look through (to)	ينظر عبر ــ ينظر من خلال
Lion	أسد		
Lioness	لبؤة	Look up (to)	ينظر إلى أعلى
Lip,	شفة	Look	نظر
List	قائمة	Lose(to-lost-	يفقد
Listen	سمع	Loss	خسارة
Literature	أدب	Lot of	كثير
Little	قليل	Lot (a)	كثير من
Little(a)	قليل من	Loud	صوت مرتفع
Live	حي	Love	حب ، عشق ــ غرام
Live	عاش	Love(to)	يحب ــ يعشق
Live (to)	يعيش ، يحيا ، يقطن	Lovely	بديع ، جميل
Liver	كبد	Low	منخفض
Living-room	صالون ــ غرفة المعيشة	Luck	حظ
		Lucky	محظوظ
Load	حمولة	Lunch	غداء
Loan	قرض ــ سلفة	Lunch(to)	يتناول الغداء
Loan (on)	مستعار ، بطريقة الاستعارة	Lung	رئة
Local call	مكالمة محلية	**M**	
Local	محلي	Machine	ماكينة ، آلة
Lock(to)	يغلق ، يقفل	Madam	سيدة
Locked	مغلق ــ مقفل	Magazine	مجلة
Lonely	وحيد ، منفرد	Magic	سحر
Long way (a)	طريق طويل	Maid	خادمة
		Mail	خطابات

Main door	المدخل الرئيسي	Mean	عنى
Main	رئيسي	Mean(to)-meant-	يعني
Make to	عمل	Meaning	معنى
Make up	جهز	Measles	حصبة
Make up(to)	يجمل الوجه بالمساحيق	Measure (to)	قاس
Make	سوي	Measures	مقاييس
Make(to)-made-	يصنع ، يعمل	Meat	لحم
Man, men	رجل ، رجال	Medical	طبي
Manager	مدير	Meet (to)	قابل
Many	كثير	Meet (to)-met	يقابل
Map	خريطة	Meeting	حفلة / اجتماع
Mark	درجة ، علامة	Melon	شمام
Mark(to)	علم ــ وضع علامة	Mend to	رف
Market	سوق	Menu	قائمة الطعام
Marketing manager	مدير التسويق	Message	رسالة
Married	متزوج	Middle	وسط
Marry(to)-married-	يتزوج	Mild	خفيف
Marvel	أعجوبة ، معجزة	Milk	حليب
Marvelous	رائع ، عجيب	Mineral water	ماء معدنية
Master, mistress	سيد ــ صاحب ــ مالك	Minister	وزير
Match	مباراة ، عود ثقاب	Ministry	وزارة
Match(to)	يوفق	Minute	دقيقة
Matching	ناسب	Mirror	مرائية
Mathematics	الرياضيات	Miss	آنسة
Matter(to)	يهم ، يحدث	Missing	ناقص
Matter(what is the)	ما الأمر	Mistake	خطأ
May-might-	يستطيع	Mister	سيد
Meal	وجبة	Mobile	نقال / جوال
		Mode of payment	طريقة الدفع
		Monday	يوم الاثنين
		Money	نقود

Month	شهر	Night	ليل
Monthly	شهري	No objection	لا مانع
Moon	قمر	Noon	ظهر
More	اكثر	North	شمال
Morning	صباح	Nose	انف
Mother	والدة	Not	غير
Mountain	جبل	Note	ورقة
Moustache	شنب	Nothing	لا شيء
Mouth	فم	Notice	تنبيه
Move	حرك	Notify	بلغ
Movement	لحظة	Number	رقم
Mrs.	سيدة	Nurse	ممرض / ممرضة
Municipality	بلدية	Nuts	مكسرات
Museum	متحف		
Must	لازم / لا بد		

N

O

Nail	ظفر	Oasis	واحة
Name	اسم	Occupied	مشغول
Napkin	فوطة	Office boy	فراش
Narrow	ضيق	Office	مكتب
Natural	طبيعي	Officer	ضابط
Naval	رقبة	Oil	زيت
Near	قريب	Old	عجوز
Necessary	ضروري	On	على
Necklace	عقد	Onion	بصل
Need to	احتاج	Only	فقط
Needle	إبرة	Open	مفتوح
Nerve	عصب	Operation	عملية
Never	أبدا	Operator	مشغل
New	جديد	Opposite	ضد
News paper	جريدة	Or	أو
		Orange	برتقال
		Orchestra	فرقة

Order	طلب	People	ناس
Oriental	شرقي	Percent	في المائة
Other	آخر	Performance	عرض
Outside	خارج	Perfume	عطر
Oven	فرن	Perhaps	ربما
		Period	مدة

P

		Permission	ترخيص
Pain	ألم	Person	شخص
Painkiller	مهدئ	Pharmacist	صيدلي
Painter	رسام	Photo	صورة
Pair	زوج	Photographer	مصور
Palace	قصر	Photography	تصور
Pants	بنطلون	Piece	قطعة
Paper	ورق	Pigeon	حمام
Paradise	جنة	Pill	حبة
Parcel	طرد	Pilot	طيار
Pardon	عفو	Pin	دبوس
Parents	والدين	Pine apple	أناناس
Park	حديقة	Pink	وردي
Participate	اشتراك	Place	مكان
Party	حفلة	Plain	سهل
Passing	مر	Plane	طائرة
Passport	جواز سفر	Play to	لعب
Past	صمغ	Play	مسرحية
Pastry	حلويات	Please call	يرجى الاتصال
Patch to	رقع	after wards	فيما بعد
Path	سكة	Please	من فضلك
Patient	مريض	Pocket	جيب
Pattern	شكل	Point to	حدد
Pay	دفع	Poison	سم
Pearl	لولي	Police	شرطة
Pencil	قلم رصاص		

Pond	بركة	**R**	
Port	ميناء	Rabbit	أرنب
Porter	شيال	Radio	راديو، مذياع
Portion	مقدار	Railway	السكة الحديد
Possible	ممكن	Rain	مطر
Post man	ساعي بريد	Rain(to)	تمطر
Post office	مكتب بريد	Raincoat	معطف المطر
Post stamp	طابع	Rainy	ممطر
Post	خطاب	Raise(to)	يرفع
Pound	جنيه	Rarely	نادرا
Practice	عادة	Rate	سعر
Prefer to	فضل	Rather	على الأصح،بالأحرى
Preference	تفضيل	Reach(to)	يصل
Pregnant	حامل	Read (to)-read-	يقرأ
Prepare	جهز	Reading	قراءة
Prescribe	كتب	Ready	مستعد / جاهز
President	رئيس	Real	حقيقي، واقعي، يقيني
Problem	حرج	Really	حقا
Producer	مخرج	Reason	سبب، داع، باعث
Q		Receipt	إيصال
Quality	نوع	Receive(to)	يستلم،يتلقى
Quantity	كمية	Recently	حديثا، مؤخرا
Quarrel (to)	يتشاجر	Reception	استقبال
Quarter	ربع	Recognise (to)	يتعرف على
Queen	ملكة	Recommend to	نصح
Question	سؤال	Record	رقم قياسي
Quick	سريع	Red	أحمر
Quickly	بسرعة	Reduction	تخفيض
Quiet	هادئ	Reflexive pronouns	الضمائر الانعكاسية
Quite	تماما ، حقا ، فعلا	Refund	استرداد

VOCABULARY

Regards	تحيات
Region	إقليم، منطقة
Register	سجل
Registration	تسجيل
Regular	عادي/قياسي
Remark (to)	يلاحظ
Remember (to)	يتذكر
Rent	إيجار
Repair	تصليح
Repair(to)	يصلح
Repeat(to)	يكرر،يعيد
Reply(to)-replied -	يجيب،يجاوب
Reporter	محرر
Representative	مندوب
Reread	يقرأ مرة ثانية
Researcher	باحث
Reservation	حجز
Residential area	منطقة السكنية
Responsible	مسئول
Rest (to)	يستريح
Rest	الباقي / راحة
Restaurant	مطعم
Return	عودة
Revision	مراجعة
Rewrite (to)-rewrote-rewritter	يكتب مرة ثانية
Ribbon	شريط
Rice	أرز
Rich	غني ، ثرى
Ride	نزهة راكبا
Right	يمين ، صحيح
Ring	خاتم

Ring(to)-rang-rung	يدق جرسا، يتحدث هاتفيا
Ringing	رنة ، رنين ،، قرع الجرس
Rise(to)-rose-risen	يقوم ، ينهض ، يشرق
River	نهر
Road help	نجدة
Road	طريق
Roar(to)roast	يزأر ، يزمجر
Roast(to)	يشوى
Room	غرفة
Rope	حبل
Rose	وردي
Round about	دوار
Royal	ملكي
Ruing	أطلال
Ruler	مسطرة

S

Safe	خزنة
Safety	أمان
Salad	سلطة
Sale	بيع
Sales representative	مندوب المبيعات
Salt	ملح
Sample	عينة
Sand	رمل
Saturday	يوم السبت
Schedule	جدول
Scientist	عالم
Scissors	مقص

155

Sculptor	نحات	Since	منذ
Seat	مكان	Sing	غني
Second hand	مستعمل	Single	عازب
Second	ثانية	Sister	أخت
Secretary	أمين	Size	مقاس
Section	قسم	Sky	سماء
Self	نفس	Sleep	نام
Sent	أرسل	Slow	بطئ
Sentence	جملة	Small	صغير
Serious	خطر	Smoke	دخن
Service	خدمة	Snakes	أكلة خفيفة
Sew	خيط	Soft	لين
Share	سهم	Soldier	عسكري
Shave	حلق	Something	نفس الشيء
Shelter	شيش	Songs	أغنية
Shin	جلد	Sorry	آسف
Ship	سفينة	Sort	صنف
Shirt	قميص	South / north	جنوب / شمال
Shop	محل	Souvenir	تذكار
Shopping centre	مركز تجاري	Speak to	كلم
Short	قصير	Speaker	سماعة
Shoulder	كتف	Special	خاص
Show	عرض	Specialist	أخصائي
Shut	مقفل	Specs	نظارات
Sick	مريض	Spend	صرف
Side	جانب	Spoon	ملعقة
Sign	وقع	Sports	رياضة
Signature	توقيع	Square	مربع
Silk	حرير	Stadium	إستاد
Silver	فضة	Staff	موظفين
Simple	سهل/ بسيط	Stain	بقعة

VOCABULARY

Stamp	طابع	Swimming pool	بركة السباحة
Star	نجم	Symptom	أعراض
Start	بدأ	Synthetic	صناعي
Station	محطة	**T**	
Statue	تمثال	Tablet	حب
Stay back	بقى	Tablet	قرص
Stay	إقامة	Tailor	خياط
Steel	سرق	Take	اخذ
Sting	قرصة	Teacher	معلم
Stitch	خيط	Team	فريق
Stomach	معدة	Tear	مزق
Stool	براز	Technician	فني
Stop	وقف	Telephone	هاتف
Strange	غريب	Tell	قال
Street	شارع	Temperature	درجة حرارة
Strong	قوي	Temporary	موقت
Student	طالب	Tent	خيمة
Study	درس	Test	امتحان
Sufficient	كافي	Thank you	شكرا على
Summer	صيف	for calling	اتصالك
Sun	شمس	Thank	شكر
Sun stoke	ضربة الشمس	That	ذلك ، تلك
Sunday	يوم الأحد	Thigh	فخذ
Suppository	لبوس	Thin	خفيف
Surcharge	رسم إضافي	Think	فكر
Surgeon	جراح	This	هذا ، هذه
Surname	لقب	Thread	خيط
Swallow	بلع	Through	من خلال
Sweat	حلو	Thursday	يوم الخميس
Swelling	ورم	Ticket	تذكرة
Swim	سبح	Tight	ضيق

Time	وقت	Uncle	عم
Time Table	جدول مواعيد	Unconscious	مغمى عليه
Tin	علبة	Under	تحت
Tire	عجلة	Understand	فهم
Tired	تعبان	University	جامعة
Today	اليوم	Until	حتى
Tomb	قبر	Up	فوق
Tomorrow	بكرة	Urgent	عاجل
Tongue	لسان	Urine	بول
Tooth paste	معجون أسنان	Use	استعمال
Tooth	سن	Useful	مفيد
Torn	ممزق	Usual	معتاد
Towards	تجاه / نحو		
Towel	فوطة	**V**	
Tower	برج	Vacant	خالي
Town	مدينة	Vacation	إجازة
Toy	لعبة	Vaccination	تطعم
Track	سكة	Valley	وادي
Trader	تاجر	Value	قيمة
Traffic	مرور	Vegetable	خضر
Train	قطار	Vein	عرق
Training	ممارسة	Vendor	بايع
Transfer	تحويل	Very	جدا
Travel	سافر	View	منظر
Treasure	خزانة	Village	قرية
Tree	شجرة	Vinegar	خل
Trip	رحلة / جولة	Visit	زيارة
Try	حاول	Visiting time	مواعيد الزيارة
Tuesday	يوم الثلاثاء	Vomit	قاء
U		**W**	
Ugly	قبيح	Wait	انتظر
Umbrella	شمسية	Waiter	جرسون

VOCABULARY

Waiting room	قاعة انتظار	Whole	كامل
Wake up	أيقظ	Why	لماذا
Wakeup	أيقظ	Wide / narrow	واسع /ضيق
Walk	مشى	Width	مساحة
Wall	حائط	Wife	زوجة
Wallet	محفظة	Wind	ريح
Want	أراد	Window	شباك
Warm	حر	Winter	شتاء
Wash	غسل	With	مع
Washing machine	غسالة	With draw	سحب
Waste basket	سلة القمامة	Without	بدون
Watch man	حارس	Woman	حرمة
Watch	ساعة	Wood	خشب
Water	ماء	Wool	صوف
Wave	موج	Word	كلمة
Way	طريق	Work	عمل
Weak	ضعيف	Worker	عامل
Weather	جو	Worst	أسوء
Wedding	زواج	Wound	جرح
Wednesday	يوم الأربعاء	Wrap to	غلف
Week	أسبوع	Write	كتب
Weekly	أسبوعي	Wrong	غلط
West	غرب		

Y

When	متى	Year	سنة
Where	أين	Yellow	أسفر
Which market do you go	أي سوق ترح	Yes	نعم
Which time	أي وقت	Yesterday	أمس
Which	أي	Yet	بعد
White	ابيض	Yield	يسلم
Who	من	Youth	شاب

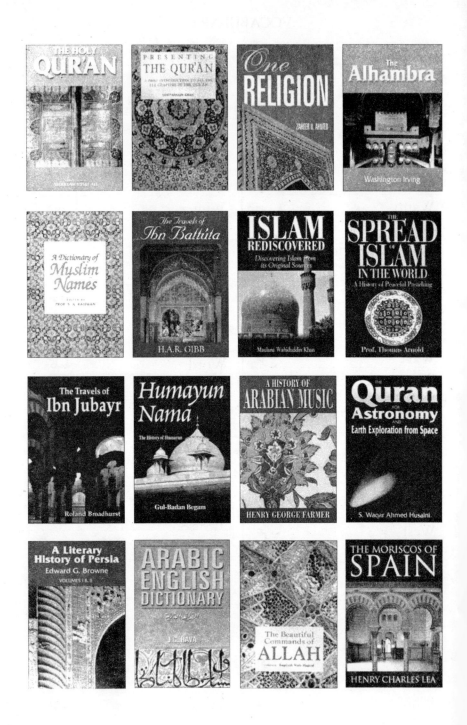